Instructor's Manual and Test Bank to Accompany

Portfolio Construction, Management and Protection

Robert A. Strong
University of Maine

West Publishing Company
Minneapolis/St. Paul   New York   Los Angeles   San Francisco

WEST'S COMMITMENT TO THE ENVIRONMENT
In 1906, West Publishing Company began recycling materials left over from the production of books. This began a tradition of efficient and responsible use of resources. Today, up to 95% of our legal books and 70% of our college texts are printed on recycled, acid-free stock. West also recycles nearly 22 million pounds of scrap paper annually—the equivalent of 181,717 trees. Since the 1960s, West has devised ways to capture and recycle waste inks, solvents, oils, and vapors created in the printing process. We also recycle plastics of all kinds, wood, glass, corrugated cardboard, and batteries, and have eliminated the use of styrofoam book packaging. We at West are proud of the longevity and the scope of our commitment to our environment.

Production, Prepress, Printing and Binding by West Publishing Company.
Cover: Painting by Jan Dorer, Waleska, GA.

COPYRIGHT © 1993 by   WEST PUBLISHING CO.
                         610 Opperman Drive
                         P.O. Box 64526
                         St. Paul, MN 55164–0526

ISBN 0–314–01885–9

CONTENTS

PART I A REVIEW OF THE BASIC PRINCIPLES OF FINANCE

   1. The Process of Portfolio Management   1
   2. The Two Key Concepts in Finance   3
   3. A Review of Statistical Principles
      Useful in Finance   11
   4. Bond Prices and the Importance of
      Duration   17

PART II PORTFOLIO CONSTRUCTION

   5. Setting Portfolio Objectives   23
   6. The Mathematics of Diversification   31
   7. Why Diversification is a Good Idea   41
   8. The Capital Markets and Market
      Efficiency   53
   9. International Investment and
      Diversification   59
 10. Picking the Equity Players   65
 11. Bond Selection   69
 12. Security Screening   73
 13. The Role of Real Assets   77

PART III PORTFOLIO MANAGEMENT

 14. Revision of the Equity Portfolio   81
 15. Revision of the Fixed Income Portfolio   87
 16. Principles of Options and Option Pricing   91
 17. Option Overwriting   97
 18. Performance Evaluation   105

PART IV PORTFOLIO PROTECTION AND EMERGING TOPICS

 19. Principles of the Futures Market   111
 20. Benching the Equity Players   117
 21. Removing Interest Rate Risk   123
 22. Integrating Derivative Assets and
      Portfolio Management   127
 23. Contemporary Issues in Portfolio
      Management   133

TESTBANK   137

NOTES ON THE SOFTWARE   237

Chapter One

The Process of Portfolio Management

KEY POINTS

Students, and instructors, often pay little attention to the first chapter in a textbook. These are often introductory pages that offer little in the way of substantive material.

This chapter, I hope, is different. It is not called an "Introduction;" it seeks to set the stage for the process of portfolio management that follows in the remaining 22 chapters.

PCMP is organized into four parts, each corresponding to one or more key steps in the portfolio management process. Chapter one highlights the topics to follow, but does not give a detailed chapter by chapter accounting.

The software is also introduced here. The sooner students begin to experiment with the two directories (Strong Software and Portman), the better. The STRONG SOFTWARE is a set of Lotus 1-2-3 templates. Most classes have some students with little or no experience with Lotus. These people should be identified early and tutoring somehow arranged. The actual Lotus competence needed to use the files is very modest, and students can be taught what they need to know in a matter of minutes.

More details on the software are enclosed elsewhere in this manual.

I use optional homework problems (one a week) each of which, if done, results in one point being added to the student's final exam score. These problems are all best solved using the software. This is a good way to get students involved outside the classroom.

Chapter Two

The Two Key Concepts in Finance

KEY POINTS

Most students taking this course will have had a prior course in basic corporate finance. Most also will have had at least one accounting class. Consequently, most of the material in this chapter should be a review. As the beginning sentence of the chapter states, Chapter 2 functions as a "crash course in the principles of finance."

Still, almost everyone will learn something from reading this chapter. There is much that instructors take for granted that shouldn't be. I find this chapter a useful way to resurrect important ideas from previous coursework and get people back into the "swing of things" before moving on to more difficult material.

TEACHING CONSIDERATIONS

The name of the game here is practice with the end of the chapter problems. Students should be encouraged to solve them using the equations presented in the chapter rather than time value of money tables. Students also should be encouraged to develop confidence in the use of a business calculator, such as the Texas Instruments BA-35 that can be acquired for less than $25.

Some material here is likely to be new, especially growing annuities, the idea of an annuity due, and the mathematics of compounding. Table 2-4 is a very handy means of generating class discussion about the nature of risk. Ask for a show of hands regarding students' preference among the four invest- ment alternatives. Be sure to elaborate on the opportunity cost issue associated with picking an investment other than choice A.

The notion of fair bets and the diminishing marginal utility of money, and the St. Petersburg paradox also are a good mechanism for prompting student involvement early in the course.

ANSWERS TO QUESTIONS

1. With simple interest the effective rate of interest will equal the nominal rate. Any compounding will cause the effective rate to exceed the nominal rate.

2. $$c_t + c_t \left[\frac{1}{R} - \frac{1}{R(1+R)^{N-1}} \right]$$

3. A future value can equal a present value only if there is no time value of money ($R = 0$). Present values exceed future values only when interest rates are negative ($R < 0$).

4. If the first payment is received immediately, it can be invested to earn interest over the first period. If it is received at the end of the period, it cannot earn interest during that first period.

5. This is best seen via a mathematical example. There is little difference between daily compounding and continuous compounding (for reasonable levels of interest rates). Monthly versus annual compounding results in the greater difference.

6. The statement is true. Consider the extremes. If $R = 0$, continuous compounding yields the same as simple interest. As R increases, the difference between simple interest and compound interest increases, too.

7. False. Utility measures the combined influences of expected return and risk. A small sum of money to be re- ceived for certain has very little utility associated with it, whereas a small investment in a very risk venture, such as a lottery ticket, has considerable utility to some people.

8. The answer depends on the individual, but many people will change their selection if the game can be played repeatedly.

9. The answer depends on the individual. Because the $50 cost is incurred despite the choice, it should not necessarily cause a person to change their selection.

10. Yes. Set the equations 2-9 and 2-11 equal to each other, cancel out the initial cash flow "C," assume some initial value for "N" or for "g" and solve for the other variable.

11. Mathematically, no, but practically speaking, yes, if the time period is long enough. Depending on the interest rate used, the present value of an annuity approaches some limit as the period increases. If the period is long enough, there is no appreciable difference in the two values.

ANSWERS TO PROBLEMS

1. Not answered here.

2. After the last payment to the custodian, the fund will have a zero balance.

So $PV_{\text{payments in}} - PV_{\text{payments out}} = 0$

Or $PV_{\text{payments in}} = PV_{\text{payments out}}$

Payments out:

$$PV = \frac{5000}{(1.08)^{26}} + \frac{5000(1.04)}{(1.08)^{27}} + \frac{5000(1.04)^2}{(1.08)^{28}} + \ldots + \frac{5000(1.04)^{14}}{(1.08)^{40}}$$

multiply both sides of the equation by $(1.08)^{26}$:

$$(1.08)^{26}\, PV = 5000 + \frac{5000(1.04)}{(1.08)} + \frac{5000(1.04)^2}{(1.08)^2} + \frac{5000(1.08)^3}{(1.08)^3} + \ldots$$

$$+ \frac{5000(1.04)^{14}}{(1.08)^{14}}$$

$$= 5000 + \frac{5000}{1.03846} + \frac{5000}{1.03846^2} + \ldots + \frac{5000}{1.03846^{14}}$$

$(1.08)^{26}$ PV = 5000 + 53356.66

$$PV = \frac{58356.66}{(1.08)^{26}} = 7889.92$$

Payments in:

let X = first payment

$$PV = X + \frac{X(1.04)}{1.08} + \frac{X(1.04)^2}{(1.08)^2} + \ldots + \frac{X(1.04)^{25}}{(1.08)^{25}}$$

$$= X + \frac{X}{1.03846} + \frac{X}{1.03846^2} + \ldots + \frac{X}{1.03846^{25}}$$

PV = X + 15.8795 X

   = 16.8795 X

Payments out = Payments in:

16.8795 X = 7889.92

X = \$467.43

3. $PV = \dfrac{100}{.12 - .05} \left[1 - (1.05/1.12)^{20} \right] = \$1,035.63$

4. $FV = PV(1 + R)^{20} = \$1,035.63 \, (1.12)^{20} = \$9,989.99$

5. $PV \times (1 + R)^t = FV$

   $(1 + R)^t = FV/PV$

   $(1 + R) = (FV/PV)^{1/t}$

   $R = (FV/PV)^{1/t} - 1$

   $R = (3,898,000/2,000,000)^{1/7} - 1 = 10.00\%$

6. $C_1 = 200$ $PV = 2500$ $g = .03$

$$PV = \frac{C_1}{R - g}$$

$$R = \frac{C_1}{PV} + g = \frac{200}{2500} + .03 = 11.00\%$$

7.

$$PV = C\left[\frac{1}{R} - \frac{1}{R(1+R)^N}\right]$$

$$FV = C\left[\frac{1}{R} - \frac{1}{R(1+R)^N}\right] \times (1 + R)^{10}$$

$$C = \frac{FV}{\left[\dfrac{1}{R} - \dfrac{1}{R(1+R)^N}\right](1 + R)^{10}}$$

$$C = \frac{50,000}{\left[\dfrac{1}{.08} - \dfrac{1}{.08(1.08)^{10}}\right](1.08)^{10}} = \$3,451.47$$

8. $PV = 1500$ $N = 18$ $C = 100$ $R = ?$

$$PV = C\left[\frac{1}{R} - \frac{1}{R(1+R)^N}\right]$$

$$\frac{PV}{100} = \left[\frac{1}{R} - \frac{1}{R(1+R)^{18}}\right] = 15$$

$R = .0199/\text{month}$

$.0199/\text{mo} \times 12 \text{ mo/yr} = 23.88\%/\text{year}$

9. $C = 1000$ $R = .06$

$$PV_4 = \frac{C}{R} = \frac{1000}{.06} = 16{,}666.67 \quad \text{(This is the value of the perpetuity at time 4.)}$$

$$PV_0 = \frac{16667.67}{(1.06)^4} = \$13{,}201.56$$

10. $PV = 200{,}000$ $R = .08$ $N = 20$ annuity due

$$200{,}000 = C + C \left[\frac{1}{.08} - \frac{1}{.08(1.08)^{19}} \right]$$

$$C = \$18{,}861.52$$

11. $9.86 + 35.59 + 31.78 = 107.22$

12. $PV = \dfrac{C_1}{R - g} = \dfrac{1.00(1.035)}{.14 - .035} = 9.86 \longrightarrow 9\ 7/8$

13. $FV = 35000$ $N = 24$ $R = .06/12 = .005$ $C = ?$

$$PV = \frac{FV}{(1 + R)^{24}} = \frac{35000}{(1.005)^{24}} = 31{,}051.50$$

$$PV = C \left[\frac{1}{R} - \frac{1}{R(1 + R)^N} \right]$$

$$C = \frac{31051.50}{\left[\dfrac{1}{.005} - \dfrac{1}{.005(1.005)^{24}} \right]}$$

$$= \frac{31051.50}{22.56} = 1{,}376.22$$

14. $PV_9 = \dfrac{C_{10}}{R - g} = \dfrac{1000}{.07 - .04} = 33,333.33$

$PV = \dfrac{PV_9}{(1 + R)^9} = \dfrac{33333.33}{(1.07)^9} = 18,131.12$

15. PV of \$50,000 annuity:

$N = 20 \qquad R = 8\% \qquad PV = 490,907.37$

PV of growing perpetuity:

$g = .04$

$PV = \dfrac{C_1}{R - g}$

$C_1 = PV(R - g) = 490907.37(.08 - .04) = \$19,636.29$

16. This is potentially a complicated problem, depending on how you view it.

Cost = construction cost + maintenance

$= 25,000 + \dfrac{500}{.12 - .05} = 32,142.86$

500 crypts:

$Return = \dfrac{benefit}{cost} = \dfrac{500X}{32142.86} = .12$

$X = \dfrac{.12\,(32142.86)}{500} = \$7.71$

To recover costs:

$\dfrac{32142.86}{500} = 64.29$ per crypt

To earn a 12% return: + 7.71 per crypt
                               ─────────
                               $72.00 per crypt

17. R = 9%   N = 10   C = 2500   PV = 16,044.14

annuity due: $PV = C + C \left[\dfrac{1}{R} - \dfrac{1}{R(1+R)^{N-1}} \right]$

$16044.14 = C + C \left[\dfrac{1}{.09} - \dfrac{1}{.09(1.09)^9} \right]$

$= C + 5.995C = 6.995C$

$C = 2293.66$

18. 264,000 miles = 264000 miles x 5280 ft/mi x 12 in/ft

$= 1.672704 \times 10^{10}$ inches

let D = number of doublings

$.004 \times 2^D = 1.672704 \times 10^{10}$

$2^D = \dfrac{1.672704 \times 10^{10}}{4.00 \times 10^{-3}} = 4.18176 \times 10^{12}$

$D = \dfrac{\ln(4.18176 \times 10^{12})}{\ln(2)} = 41.92 \quad \longrightarrow \quad 42$ doublings

19. let $x = 11.\overline{9999}$ (1)

then $10x = 119.\overline{9999}$ (2)

subtract (1) from (2):

$9x = 108.\overline{0000}$

$x = 12.\overline{0000}$

Chapter Three

A Review of Statistical Principles Useful in Finance

KEY POINTS

Like the second chapter, much of this material will be a review to some students. Some material, however, is likely to be new. Covariance and the standard error may be unfamiliar, as may R squared and the relationship between the arithmetic and geometric mean returns.

TEACHING CONSIDERATIONS

The important thing here is again to attract the student's attention by indicating that there are many underlying concepts from other courses that play a role in the portfolio management process. Statistics courses often stand alone and are often taught outside the College of Business. Ideally, statistical principles are an adjunct to the study of finance rather than being taught as an end in themselves.

This chapter shows that an understanding of these fundamentals will be useful in the pages that follow. Homework assignments from the end of chapter problems are time well spent at this early point in the course.

ANSWERS TO QUESTIONS

1. The arithmetic mean will equal the geometric mean only if all the values are identical. Any dispersion will result in the geometric mean being less than the arithmetic mean.

2. No.

3. "Return" is an intuitive idea to most people. It is most commonly associated with annual rates. Clearly 10% per year is different from 10% per week. Combining weekly and annual returns without any adjustment results in meaningless answers.

4. Returns are sometimes multiplied, and if there is an odd number of negative returns, the product is also negative. You cannot take the even root of a negative number, so it may not be possible to calculate geometric mean unless you eliminate the negative numbers by calculating return relatives first.

5. ROA divides net income by total assets; ROE divides net income by equity. ROE measures the effect of leverage on investment returns.

6. ROA, in general. ROE may be appropriate in situations where shares are bought on margin. The important thing is to ensure that comparisons are valid. Leverage adds to risk, and ideally risk should be held reasonably constant when comparing alternatives.

7. Dispersion on the positive side does not result in investment loss. Investors do not care if their investments show unusually large returns. It is only dispersion on the adverse side that results in a loss of utility.

8. The correlation between a random variable and a constant is mathematically undefined because of division by zero. (See equation 3-10.) Despite this, there are no diversification benefits associated with perfectly correlated investments. They behave as if their correlation coefficient were 1.0.

9. Semi-variance is a concept that has its advocates and its detractors. You <u>never</u> know an outcome until after the outcome has occurred, so the criticism here is a shaky one.

10. Bill only cares which team wins. Joe cares which team wins and whether they beat the spread.

11. Unless the stock is newly issued, the data are sample data from a larger population. If you have the entire history of returns, they can be considered population data.

12.   Individual stock returns are usually assumed to be from a univariate distribution.

13.   A portfolio of securities generates a return from a multivariate distribution, as the portfolio return depends on a number of subsidiary returns.

14.   The geometric mean of logreturns will be less, because logarithms reduce the dispersion.

15.   Standard deviations are calculated from the variance, which is calculated by the square of deviations about the mean.   Squaring the deviations removes negative signs.

ANSWERS TO PROBLEMS

1. $GM = \left[\prod_{i=1}^{N} x_i \right]^{1/4} = (1 \cdot 2 \cdot 3 \cdot 4 \cdot 5 \cdot 6)^{1/6} = 2.99$

2. $\bar{x} = \dfrac{1}{N} \sum_{i=1}^{N} x_i = \dfrac{1}{8}$ [.0005 + 0 − .0012 + .0001 − .0010 −

.0002 + .0011 + 0] $= \dfrac{1}{8}$ [−.0007] = −0.0000875

Week	Return	Prob	Return x prob
1	$(.0005 - \bar{x})^2$	.125	ignore
2	$(0 - \bar{x})^2$	.125	ignore
3	$(-.0012 - \bar{x})^2$	.125	2.07×10^{-7}
4	$(.0001 - \bar{x})^2$	.125	ignore
5	$(-.0010 - \bar{x})^2$	.125	1.48×10^{-7}
6	$(-.0002 - \bar{x})^2$	.125	1.03×10^{-8}
7	$(.0011 - \bar{x})^2$	.125	ignore
8	$(0 - \bar{x})^2$	.125	ignore
			3.65×10^{-7}

3. $E\left[(\tilde{x} - \bar{x})^2 \right] = E\left[\tilde{x}^2 - 2\tilde{x}\bar{x} + \bar{x}^2 \right]$ (1)

$= E(\tilde{x}^2) - 2E(\tilde{x}\bar{x}) + E(\bar{x}^2)$ (2)

$E(\tilde{x}) = \bar{x}$ (3)

$$E(\tilde{x}\bar{x}) = \bar{x}E(\tilde{x}) \tag{4}$$

$$E(\bar{x}^2) = \bar{x}^2 \tag{5}$$

substitute (4) into (2):

$$E(\tilde{x}^2) - 2\bar{x}E(\tilde{x}) + E(\bar{x}^2) \tag{6}$$

substitute (3) and (5) into 6:

$$E(\tilde{x}^2) - 2(\bar{x})^2 + \bar{x}^2 \tag{7}$$

$$= E(\tilde{x}^2) - \bar{x}^2 \tag{8}$$

4. $COV(\tilde{x}, a) = E[(\tilde{x} - \bar{x})(a - \bar{a})]$

  because "a" is a constant, $\bar{a} = a$

  therefore, $(a - \bar{a}) = 0$ and $COV(\tilde{x}), a) = 0$

5. $Y = a + b\tilde{x}$

  $\sigma^2 = E[(a + b\tilde{x}) - E(a + b\tilde{x})]^2$

  $= E[(a + b\tilde{x}) - a - b\bar{x})]^2$

  $= E[a + b\tilde{x} - a + b\tilde{x}]^2$

  $= E[b\tilde{x} - b\bar{x}]^2$

  $= E[b(\tilde{x} - \bar{x})]^2$

  $= b^2 E[(\tilde{x} - \bar{x})]^2$

  $= b^2 \sigma^2$

6. $COV(a\tilde{x}, \tilde{y}) = E[(a\tilde{x} - E(a\tilde{x}))(\tilde{y} - E(\tilde{y}))]$

  $= E[(a\tilde{x} - aE(\tilde{x}))(\tilde{y} - E(\tilde{y}))]$

  $= aE[(\tilde{x} - E(\tilde{x}))(\tilde{y} - E(\tilde{y}))$

  $= aE[(\tilde{x} - \bar{x})(\tilde{y} - \bar{y})]$

  $= aCOV(\tilde{x}, \tilde{y})$

7.	week	return	return relative	logreturn
	1	0.0005	1.0005	5.00×10^{-4}
	2	0	1.0000	0
	3	- 0.0012	0.9988	-1.20×10^{-3}
	4	0.0001	1.0001	1.00×10^{-4}
	5	- 0.0010	0.9990	-1.00×10^{-3}
	6	- 0.0002	0.9998	-2.00×10^{-4}
	7	0.0011	1.0011	1.10×10^{-3}
	8	0	1.0000	0

8.   a) returns: GM = 0.9999
     b) logreturns: GM = 0.9999

9.	observation	$\tilde{x}$	$2\tilde{x}$	$(2\tilde{x} - \bar{x})^2$
	1	2	4	1.96
	2	-1	-2	21.16
	3	4	8	29.16
	4	1	2	0.36
	5	2	4	1.96
	6	-2	-4	43.56
	7	5	10	54.76
	8	-1	-2	21.16
	9	0	0	6.76
	10	3	6	11.56
			$\bar{x}$ = 2.6	192.40

$$192.40 \div 10 = 19.24$$

$$4.81 \times 2^2 = 19.24$$

10.   standard error $= \dfrac{\sigma}{\sqrt{n}} = \dfrac{6.97 \times 10^{-4}}{\sqrt{8}} = 2.46 \times 10^{-4}$

Chapter Four

Bond Prices and the Importance of Duration

KEY POINTS

Much of the material in this chapter will be a review to the better student. As with the previous chapters, it should be useful to almost everyone to read this material again. The important thing is that trivial aspects of bonds (such as the dollar amount of interest a 7% coupon bond pays annually) should be no-brainers.

There is much terminology here, and students may need some prodding to learn it all. The test bank has over 70 questions from this chapter; this is sometimes sufficient motivation to get them to go over the material carefully.

Dealing with semi-annual compounding is another important point in this chapter, as is the reinvestment rate assumption associated with the bond's yield to maturity. Stress that it is not possible to "lock in" a yield to maturity with a bond that pays periodic interest.

TEACHING CONSIDERATIONS

Some instructors may want to assign some outside reading regarding theories of the yield curve. The end of the chapter references contain some good candidates.

It is also important to ensure that accrued interest gets covered and understood here. This will become important in later chapters as portfolios are built and you seek to avoid overspending.   Spend some time on the difference between interest rate risk and reinvestment rate risk.

Duration should be introduced as a concept here.   It will be dealt with in greater detail later in the book.   Show that it has two definitions: 1) a measure of interest rate risk (incorporating Malkiel's theorems), and 2) the weighted average of time until the bond's cash flows occur.

Consider assigning a homework problem using the DURATION file from the Strong Software disk.

ANSWERS TO QUESTIONS

1.   No.   As the cash flows are not known for certain, the yield to maturity cannot be calculated.

2.   If the two securities have the same coupon, the same degree of default risk, and the same remaining time until maturity, they should sell for exactly the same price because the market considers them identical securities.

3.   The statement is true, everything else being equal.

4.   Treasury bonds have an initial life of more than 10 years.   Treasury notes have an initial life of up to 10 years.

5.   Convenience risk refers to the possibility of "loss" due to added managerial time necessary to properly manage the portfolio.

6.   Bonds sometimes sell at a premium, in which case the bond will be redeemed at a loss if called.   Capital gains are also determined relative to your purchase price, which may be more or less than the call price.   The call also may involve managerial inconvenience that outweighs any call premium or capital gain.

7.   If the interest rates associated with all maturities move up or down by the same amount, this is a parallel shift. This assumes, for instance, that if T bill rates rise by one half point, so do 30 year bond rates.

8.   Arbitrage is present if a convertible bond sells for less than its conversion value.   If it did, people would buy the bond, convert it, sell the shares, and have more money than when they started (ignoring transaction costs).

9. $20 per ounce: $1000 par ÷ 50 ounces

10.   Accrued interest must be paid when the bond is purchased and is received when the bond is sold.   This amount is in actual dollars and is reflected on trade confirmation slips.

11.   The rating change from A to BBB represents an increase in default risk; as a consequence, the bond price will fall and the bond yield will increase.

12.   The realized compound yield is the same as the yield to maturity when interest is assumed to have been compounded semi-annually.

13.   This is because of reinvestment rate risk and because future reinvestment rates are not known.

14.   The convertible bond's conversion value.

15.   Companies issue convertible bonds largely because they hope never to have to pay them off.   The firm wants the bondholder to convert, likes to see the number of shareholders grow, and is not interested in having the debt reappear on the books.   This could wreck havoc with other debt covenants and make short term financial planning difficult.

16.   There is no way to make a riskless dollar.   Buying the bond, converting it, and selling the stock would leave you with less money than when you started.

ANSWERS TO PROBLEMS

1.   <u>Five year</u>:

$$FV = PV(1 + R/2)^{2N}$$

$$= \$1000(1 + .09/2)^{10} = \$1,552.97$$

$$\text{interest} = FV - PV = \$1,552.97 - \$1,000 = \$552.97$$

<u>4.5 Year</u>:

$$FV = \$1,000(1 + .095/2)^{9} = \$1,518.40$$

$$\text{interest} = \$1,518.40 - \$1,000 = \$518.40$$

difference = $552.97 - 518.40 = $34.57

2.   Assume semi-annual interest:

$$P_0 = \sum_{t=1}^{14} \frac{40}{(1 + .095/2)^t} + \frac{1000}{(1 + .0915/2)^{14}} = \$941.50$$

3.   a. $D = \dfrac{\left[\displaystyle\sum_{t=1}^{14} \dfrac{40}{(1 + .0915/2)^2} \cdot t \right] + \dfrac{1000}{(1 + .0915/2)^2} \cdot 14}{941.50}$

= 5.44 years

b. $D = \dfrac{40 \left[\dfrac{(1+.0915/2)^{15} - (1+.0915/2) - \dfrac{.0915 \cdot 14}{2}}{(.0915/2)^2\,(1 + .0915/2)^{14}}\right] + \dfrac{1000 \cdot 14}{(1.0915/2)^{14}}}{941.50}$

$$= 40 \left[\frac{1.956 - 1.046 - .641}{.002\,(1.871)}\right] + \frac{1000\,(14)}{1.04575^{14}}$$

= 10.81 periods = 5.41 years

4.   N = 8 P_0 = 500   FV = 1000

a.   Using Rule of 72:   the value doubles in 8 years;
72/8 = 9%

b.   PV $= \dfrac{FV}{(1+R)^t}$ $(1+R)^t = \dfrac{FV}{PV}$ $R = (FV/PV)^{1/t} - 1$

$R = 2^{(1/8)} - 1 = 9.05\%$

Using semi-annual periods:

$R = 2^{(1/16)} - 1 = 4.43;$ 4.43 x 2 = 8.86%

5. a. $$800 = \sum_{t=1}^{7} \frac{80}{(1+R)^t} + \frac{1000}{(1+R)^7} \qquad R = 12.44\%$$

    b. $$800 = \sum_{t=1}^{14} \frac{40}{(1+R/2)^t} + \frac{1000}{(1+R/2)^{14}} \qquad R = 12.73\%$$

6. 7 1/4% ==> $$\frac{.0725 \times \$1000}{365} = \$0.1986/day$$

    $0.1986 x 43 = $8.54

7. first solve for R: R = 10.74%

    PV of annuity: $$\sum_{t=1}^{42} \frac{75/2}{(1+(.1046/2))^t} = 632.75$$

    PV of principal: $$\frac{1000}{(1+(.1046/2))^{42}} = 117.53$$

    Interest: 632.75/750 = 84.3%

    Principal: 100% - 84.3% = 15.7%

8. (The bond sells for par.)   D = 17.67

9. Use equation 4-6:

    $$\text{Effective annual rate} = \left[1 + (R/X)\right]^X - 1$$

    $$= \left[1 + .135/12\right]^{12} - 1 = 14.37\%$$

10. $$\text{Conversion ratio} = \frac{\text{par value}}{\text{conv. price}} = \frac{1000}{9.54} = 104.82 \text{ shares}$$

11.   Conversion value = conversion ratio x stock price

$$= 104.82 \times \$10 = \$1048.20$$

12.   Premium over conversion value = bond price - conversion value

$$\$1100 - \$1048.20 = \$51.80$$

13 - 14.   Omitted

15.   Smith has a <u>compound</u> yield of 10%; Jones has a <u>simple</u> yield of 10%.

16.   Accrued interest paid:

$$5 \times 39 \text{ days} \times 70/365 = (37.40)$$

interest received: 175.00

Accrued interest received:

$$31 \times 5 \times 70/365 = \qquad 29.73$$

$$\underline{\qquad\qquad}$$

$$\$167.33$$

17.   a.   The point here is that once the short term bond matures there is a reinvestment rate issue. You cannot calculate a portfolio yield to maturity when maturities do not coincide.

      b.   If both bonds have the same maturity and market rates equal 10.5%

18.   Omitted.

Chapter Five

Setting Portfolio Objectives

KEY POINTS

This topic is extremely important, yet receives little attention in the existing textbooks. The process of setting objectives can be difficult because of issues with semantics, with someone's difficulty in making a decision, or because of the subjective nature of investment goals.

Time spent in the objective setting process invariably makes the finished product a better one, and helps both the portfolio manager and the beneficiary become more intimate with the investment package.

The importance of primary and secondary objectives is a key point of this chapter, as is the fact that certain primary/secondary objective combinations are infeasible. Risk and expected return go hand in hand.

Portfolio dedication using cash matching or duration matching is a useful portfolio management tool introduced here. These techniques indicate the technical, and analytic, nature of the portfolio management process to be discussed in the coming weeks.

TEACHING CONSIDERATIONS

Give good coverage to the merits of the _growth_ _of_ _income_ objective. This is frequently the most appropriate objective for endowment funds and public trust funds. An understanding

of the merits of such an objective helps breed confidence in
· the student. The distinction between income and growth of
income is extremely important. Use Figure 5-1. Figure 5-2
shows classical Ibbotson and Sinquefield results generally
consistent with the linear relationship between risk and
return, although the fact that intermediate government bonds
have outperformed long-term bonds remains an anomaly.

In discussing duration matching, stress the trade-off
between interest rate risk and reinvestment rate risk, and
the fact that in a duration matched portfolio the two effects
will cancel out. Rising interest rates will reduce the value
of the portfolio, but the higher interest earned on reinvested funds will offset the loss.

An important distinction between cash matching and duration matching is that a duration-matched portfolio is often
"used up" at the end of the investment horizon. That is, the
fund is gone at the end of the period. A cash-matched portfolio, on the other hand, often keeps the principal intact
over the period, only relying on the generation of income for
the payment of obligations.

ANSWERS TO QUESTIONS

1.   The income objective generates a generally consistent
level of income from the portfolio. Higher levels of income
can be achieved by investing in higher risk securities. The
growth of income objective initially accepts a lower level of
income because of some investment in equity securities. As
time passes, the equity securities normally appreciate,
thereby increasing the principal value of the portfolio, and
enabling additional funds to be invested in income-producing
securities.

2.   Secondary objectives help find the percentage of the fund
that should be invested in equity securities.

3.   Try to figure out what the income is needed for: retirement income, a supplement to retirement income, funds to
augment an organization's operating budget, etc. Also,
determine the length of time the income will need to be
generated. An 80 year old person would be more likely suited
to an income objective generating level income, whereas a
recently retired 65 year old would probably want to seek
increasing retirement income via a growth of income objective.

4. None. No. Common stock is inappropriate when stability of principal is either the primary or the secondary objective.

5. No. Yield can always be increased by investing in riskier securities (bonds, most likely), but the purchase of a portfolio of CC-rated bonds is not likely always to be the prudent thing to do.

6. One set of factors includes subjective matters that the client might suggest, such as a desire to invest locally or a desire to avoid certain industries. The size of the portfolio also may dictate the number of different issues that should be selected. In general, it is a good idea to avoid placing too great a percentage of the portfolio's funds in any single security.

7. Technically, this statement is true. Some clients, however, will not understand duration, and if they choose to focus on maturity instead, you should be able to deal with the fact.

8. Many people agree with this. There is a difference in risk, however small, and whether it is material is a matter of opinion. Some portfolios may be prohibited from investing in a bond that is not AAA rated, too.

9. Income comes from current yield; it is more important in this situation.

10. Zero coupon bonds could be used with the capital appreciation objective and conceivably with the growth of income.

11. No.

12. There is no reason certificates of deposit are inconsistent with a stability of income objective.

13. There is reinvestment rate risk, but ideally it will be offset by the effects of interest rate risk.

14. Investment policy is a long-term concept; investment strategy comprises the short-term steps taken that are consistent with investment policy.

15.   There is some truth to this.   Duration matching does
require the use of principal to provide income in some cir-
cumstances.

16.   This involves some personal preference, but many people
would recommend a combination of capital appreciation and
growth of income.   Others who are more conservative would
prefer growth of income and income.   Still others would
choose income and stability of principal.

17.   The issue of whether the SSA should be able to invest in
equity securities would be useful classroom discussion.   If
it cannot, it is limited to <u>income</u> and <u>stability</u> <u>of</u> <u>princi-</u>
<u>pal</u>.

18.   The results are an anomaly with no obvious explanation.

ANSWERS TO PROBLEMS

1.   The portfolio must generate $50,000 every September 1.
All four bonds in Table 5-6 pay interest on September 1, so
any or all four of them can be used.   One simple solution
would be to buy 500 of the JKL bonds.   They have a 10% coupon,   meaning that they generate $50,000 per year in   income.

Because the bonds pay semi-annually, you can reinvest the
first coupon proceeds until they are needed.   If you assume
that you can reinvest at the coupon rate of 10%, each bond
actually generates $102.50 each year.   This means you only
need 488 bonds.   They would generate $24,400 in interest
twice, plus you would earn $1,220 on the reinvestment of the
first interest check.

2.   First, find the present value of the $50,000 twenty year
annuity.   At 10%, the answer is $425,678.   Next, find the
duration of this annuity.   This is easiest using the closed-
form equation: the answer is 7.50.   Then find a package of
the bonds that has this duration and this market value.

    I solved this using a SAS linear program.   One solution
(rounded to the nearest bond) is to use 162 of the ABC bonds
and 261 of the GHI bonds.

3. $9000 = 7000 \times (1.04)^t$ Solve for t.

$$9000/7000 = (1.04)^t$$

$$1.2857 = (1.04)^t$$

$$\ln (1.2857) = t \ln (1.04)$$

$$t = \frac{\ln (1.2857)}{\ln (1.04)} = 6.41$$

4. Compare the three present values:

a. PV of annuity @ 8%, 12 years, C = $55,000: $414,484

b. PV of growing annuity @ 8%, C = $55,000 x .85, g = 5%: $446,993

c. PV of lump sum = $400,000

The growing annuity has the highest present value.

5. A higher discount rate can change the preferred alternative. In this case, the new present values are:

a. $298,134

b. $310,580

c. $400,000

Clearly, the lump sum is now preferable.

6. As the text suggests, the BONDPORT file on the Strong Software disk is helpful in solving this problem. The problem here is to compare the monthly income needs with the income expected to be generated by an existing portfolio.

Sample printouts from the BONDPORT file are enclosed. These show the par value, coupon and maturity of each bonds in Table 5-7, with the months in which they pay interest. Yield to maturity and duration are not needed for this problem, so these columns have been left blank. (To fill them in, students would need the DURATION file.)

The "schedule of income receipts" printout shows the monthly totals received from the bonds. The printout entitled "Income Forecast for 1991" (from a separate Lotus 1-2-3 worksheet) shows the end of the month cash balance after receipt of the bond income and the payment of the monthly check to the church. By finding the maximum shortfall over the year, this amount can be transferred the first time any

INCOME FORECAST FOR 1991

	DEC 90	JAN	FEB	MAR	APR	MAY	JUN	JUL	AUG	SEP	OCT	NOV	DEC
+ Cash Receipts		3025	1200	0	1223	9704	2763	3025	1200	0	1223	9704	2763
- Cash Disbursements		4778	4778	4778	4778	4778	4778	4778	4778	4778	4778	4778	4778
+ Transfers from Equity				17417									
= Cash on Hand	7000	5247	1669	14308	10753	15679	13664	11911	8333	3555	0	4926	2911

SCHEDULE OF INCOME RECEIPTS

[for bonds at left]	ISSUE		JAN JUL	FEB AUG	MAR SEP	APR OCT	MAY NOV	JUN DEC
$25,000	FMC	8.75%94	0	0	0	0	1094	0
$40,000	VEP	9.38%98	0	0	0	0	0	1875
$30,000	FHLB	8.15%92	0	0	0	1223	0	0
$25,000	FHLB	8.60%92	0	0	0	0	1075	0
$15,000	FHLB	8.80%92	0	0	0	0	660	0
$30,000	FHLB	9.50%93	1425	0	0	0	0	0
$40,000	FHLB	10.75%93	0	0	0	0	2150	0
$40,000	US	8.00%94	1600	0	0	0	0	0
$20,000	FHLB	8.88%95	0	0	0	0	0	888
$50,000	FNMA	9.35%97	0	0	0	0	2338	0
$50,000	FNMA	9.55%97	0	0	0	0	2388	0
$30,000	US	8.00%99	0	1200	0	0	0	0

Monthly totals: $3,025 $1,200 $0 $1,223 $9,704 $2,763

ALT S for bond portfolio main menu

BOND PORTFOLIO
ALT S for bond portfolio main menu

par	issue	coupon	maturity	Price	Market Value	Ytm	Current Yield	Dur.
$25,000	FMC	8.750%	1994	104.375	$26,094		8.38%	
40,000	VEP	9.375%	1998	111	$44,400		8.45%	
30,000	FHLB	8.150%	1992	101.312	$30,394		8.04%	
25,000	FHLB	8.600%	1992	101.734	$25,434		8.45%	
15,000	FHLB	8.800%	1992	103.859	$15,579		8.47%	
30,000	FHLB	9.500%	1993	105.078	$31,523		9.04%	
40,000	FHLB	10.750%	1993	107.906	$43,162		9.96%	
40,000	US	8.000%	1994	107	$42,800		7.48%	
20,000	FHLB	8.875%	1995	110.281	$22,056		8.05%	
50,000	FNMA	9.350%	1997	112.671	$56,336		8.30%	
50,000	FNMA	9.550%	1997	115.469	$57,735		8.27%	
30,000	US	8.000%	1999	108.406	$32,522		7.38%	

$395,000   PORTFOLIO TOTALS $428,034   8.37% 0.00

Market value as percentage of par =   108.36%

shortfall occurs, eliminating the need to transfer funds
again during the year. Here, a transfer of $17,417 in March
results in a zero cash balance in October.

Ideally, it is not a good idea for the cash balance to
fall all the way to zero, so the actual transfer perhaps
should be higher. Also, there will be some interest earned
on idle funds that is not considered here.

Planning for 1992 can occur the same way, with the $60,196
target allocated over the twelve months and shortfalls noted.
It will again be necessary to transfer funds from the stock
portfolio to meet the income constraint. During 1992 there
also will be bonds maturing; they will need to be replaced,
and at an uncertain rate.

The actual solution to this problem also resulted in the
$4,000 interest on the mortgage being transferred to princi-
pal so that some maturing principal could be transferred to
income.

Chapter Six

The Mathematics of Diversification

KEY POINTS

The mathematics of diversification are intimidating to some students, largely because the nature of the equations is unfamiliar. The summation sign, especially double summation signs like in equation 6-2, may be imposing.

The principal points of this chapter are: 1) the expected return of a linear combination is a weighted average of the component expected returns, and 2) the variance of a linear combination is _not_ a simple weighted average of the component variances.

Other key topics include the idea of a minimum variance portfolio, the important role of return correlation, and the concept of covariance. Finally, the utility of the single index model is mentioned, particularly how it facilitates the computation of portfolio statistics.

TEACHING CONSIDERATIONS

Be sure to incorporate the COV and MINVAR files from the Strong Software disk into your discussion of this material. A good homework assignment is to provide students with a set of returns on two stocks and ask them to figure out the minimum variance portfolio. This requires using the COV file to get the two variances and the correlation of returns, and then using the MINVAR file to incorporate these statistics into determination of the minimum variance portfolio.

I do not require students to memorize any formulae from
this chapter except equations 6-1 and 6-8. I know some
instructors will feel differently about this, and depending
on teaching style, there is some value in the other approach.
It is a matter of personal preference, I think.

It may help relieve some anxiety to show that chapter
seven builds upon chapter six, and that additional clarity
comes from this next chapter. It is better to give an exam
after chapter seven rather than after chapter six.

ANSWERS TO QUESTIONS

1. Selling stock short brings cash in rather than requiring
a cash outflow. In the absence of margin requirements (which
is arguably true for large institutional investors), this
means there is no initial investment, and any gain on no
investment is an infinite return.

2. omitted

3. The two-security portfolio is preferable, as it has
higher expected return per unit of risk.

4. Covariance is the expected value of the product of two
numbers. Each of the two numbers is a value minus its mean.
Some values lie below the mean, some above. Consequently,
each number can be positive or negative, and the product can
therefore be positive or negative. Depending on the nature
of the dispersions around the means, the expected value of
the product can be positive or negative.

5. $E[(\tilde{a}-\bar{a})(\tilde{b}-\bar{b})] = COV(\tilde{a},\tilde{b})$ and $E[(\tilde{b}-\bar{b})(\tilde{a}-\bar{a})] = COV(\tilde{b},\bar{a})$.
By the commutative law for multiplication, $ab = ba$. This
means the order of the two products inside the expected value
operator can be reversed and $COV(\tilde{a},\tilde{b}) = COV(\tilde{b},\tilde{a})$.

6. $\beta_a = \tau_{am}\ \sigma_a\ \sigma_m$

where τ_{am} = correlation between security a and the
                market
       σ_a = standard deviation of security a
       σ_m = standard deviation of the market

7. $0.25 \times (4)^{.5} \times (6)^{.5} = 1.225$

8. The size of the error term approaches zero as the number of portfolio components increases.

9. Standard deviations can only be positive, so a negative correlation means the covariance is also negative.

10. In a prediction model, R squared can only increase if additional explanatory variables are added. You cannot lose predictive ability by including additional data.

ANSWERS TO PROBLEMS

1. $(n^2 - n)/2 = (1700^2 - 1700)/2 = 1,444,150$

2.

$$X_A = \frac{\sigma_B^2 - \sigma_A \sigma_B \tau_{AB}}{\sigma_A^2 + \sigma_B^2 - 2\sigma_A \sigma_B \tau_{AB}}$$

$$= \frac{.28 - (.23)^{.5}(.28)^{.5} \tau_{AB}}{.23 + .28 - 2(.23)^{.5}(.28)^{.5} \tau_{AB}}$$

$$\tau_{AB} = \frac{COV(\tilde{A},\tilde{B})}{\sigma_A \sigma_B} = \frac{.047}{(.23)^{.5}(.28)^{.5}} = 0.185$$

$$X_A = \frac{.28 - (.23)^{.5}(.28)^{.5}(.185)}{.23 + .28 - 2(.23)^{.5}(.28)^{.5}(.185)}$$

$$= \frac{0.233}{0.416} = 56.0\%$$

$$X_B = 1 - X_A = 1 - 56.0\% = 44.0\%$$

3. $\beta_p = \sum_{i=1}^{4} x_i \beta_i = \frac{1}{4}(1.05 + 1.20 + 0.90 + 0.95) = 1.025$

4. $\sigma_p^2 = \beta_p^2 \sigma^2 + \sigma_{ep}^2$

The error term approaches zero, so

$\sigma_p^2 = (1.025)^2 (.25) = 0.263$

5. $X_A = -.30 \quad X_B = .50 \quad X_C = .80$

$$E(\tilde{R}_p) = \sum_{i=1}^{N} x_i E(\tilde{R}_i)$$

$$= (-.30)(.14) + (.50)(.16) + (.80)(.12) = .0134 = 13.4\%$$

$$\sigma_p^2 = \sum_{i=1}^{N} \sum_{j=1}^{N} x_i x_j \tau_{ij} \sigma_i \sigma_j$$

$$= X_A^2 \sigma_A^2 + X_B^2 \sigma_B^2 + X_C^2 \sigma_C^2 + X_A X_C \tau_{AC} \sigma_A \sigma_C + X_A X_B \tau_{AB} \sigma_A \sigma_B +$$

$$X_B X_C \tau_{BC} \sigma_B \sigma_C$$

$$= (-.3)^2(.23) + (.5)^2(.28) + (.8)^2(.21)$$

$$+ (-.3)(.8)\tau_{AC}(.23)^{.5}(.21)^{.5} +$$

$$(-.3)(.5)\tau_{AB}(.23)^{.5}(.28)^{.5} +$$

$$(.5)(.8)\tau_{BC}(.28)^{.5}(.21)^{.5}$$

$$= .0207 + .07 + .1344 - .0527\tau_{AC} - .0381\tau_{AB} + .0444\tau_{BC}$$

$$\tau_{AB} = \frac{COV(\tilde{A},\tilde{B})}{\sigma_A \ \sigma_B} = \frac{.047}{(.23)^{.5}(.28)^{.5}} = 0.185$$

$$\tau_{AC} = \frac{COV(\tilde{A},\tilde{C})}{\sigma_A \ \sigma_C} = \frac{.062}{(.23)^{.5}(.21)^{.5}} = 0.282$$

$$\tau_{BC} = \frac{COV(\tilde{B},\tilde{C})}{\sigma_B \ \sigma_C} = \frac{.051}{(.28)^{.5}(.21)^{.5}} = 0.210$$

$$\sigma_p^2 = .0207 + .07 + .1344 - .0527(.282) - .0381(.185)$$
$$+ .0444(.210) = 0.2125$$

6. $\sigma_{CD} = \beta_C \, \beta_D \, \sigma_m^2$

$$\sigma_m^2 = \frac{\sigma_{CD}}{\beta_C \, \beta_D} = \frac{0.063}{(.90)(.95)} = .074$$

7. $\sigma^2 = 25\% = .25$

$\sigma = (.25)^{.5} = .5 = 50\%$

8. $\tau_{BC} = \dfrac{COV(\check{B}, \check{C})}{\sigma_B \sigma_C} = \dfrac{.051}{(.28)^{.5}(.21)^{.5}} = .210$

9. $\sigma_{12} = \beta_1 \, \beta_2 \, \sigma_m^2$

$$\sigma_m^2 = \frac{\sigma_{12}}{\beta_1 \, \beta_2} = \frac{1.55}{1.10 \times 1.25} = 1.127$$

10. See attached computer sheets.

$E(\check{R}_p) = .30(-.15\%) + .70(1.19\%) = 0.788\%$

From the graph, $\sigma_p^2 \approx 0.0008$

11. See attached sheet.

$E(\check{R}) = 0.0041 \qquad \sigma_p^2 = 0.0005$

12. Omitted.

13. Omitted.

COVARIANCE FILE

This file calculates the standard deviation and mean return of up to five securities, with up to 100 observations for each security. The COVARIANCE MATRIX and CORRELATION MATRIX are also calculated. This information is necessary for the calculation of the efficient frontier or for determining the total risk of a portfolio.

You must input the same number of returns for each security.

After inputting data, make sure the CALC light in the lower part of the screen is out; hit F9 if it isn't.

Hit the ALT key and S simultaneously to return to the main menu.

PAGE DOWN TO BEGIN INPUTTING DATA
(or hit ALT S for main menu)

ENTER UP TO 100 RETURNS FOR UP TO FIVE SECURITIES
IN LOTUS COLUMNS B, C, D, E, AND F

You must
the same
of observ
for each

HIT ESC to enter data or ALT S for menu.

you inclu

Return #	sec1	sec2	sec3	sec4	sec5	<--input
EXAMPLE	10.00%	-8.00%	20.00%	10.00%	0.00%	
1	0.0270	-0.0230	0.0560	0.0020	0.0330	
2	0.0120	0.0000	0.0130	0.0040	0.0170	
3	-0.0220	-0.0100	-0.0150	0.0020	-0.0450	
4	0.0130	0.0340	0.0150	0.0100	0.0080	
5	-0.0110	-0.0230	0.0120	-0.0290	-0.0190	
6	-0.0330	-0.0610	-0.0350	-0.0220	-0.0240	
7	0.0290	0.0260	0.0020	0.0000	-0.0010	
8	0.0550	0.0450	0.0470	0.0200	0.0560	
9						

PROBLEM 6-10

Security Statistics

	sec1	sec2	sec3	sec4	sec5
mean	0.88%	-0.15%	1.19%	-0.16%	0.31%
std dev	0.02736	0.03301	0.02786	0.01512	0.03054
variance	7.49E-04	1.09E-03	7.76E-04	2.28E-04	9.33E-04

CORRELATION MATRIX

	sec1	sec2	sec3	sec4	sec5
sec1	1.000				
sec2	0.781	1.000			
sec3	0.824	0.481	1.000		
sec4	0.739	0.792	0.534	1.000	
sec5	0.901	0.545	0.853	0.640	1.000

PROBLEM 6-10

DETERMINING THE MINIMUM VARIANCE
TWO-SECURITY PORTFOLIO

Enter the appropriate information in column C:

Variance of Stock A: 0.0011   (Standard deviation = 0.0330)

Variance of Stock B: 0.0008   (Standard deviation = 0.0279)

Correlation between   For diversification benefits,
Stocks A and B: 0.4810   the correlation coefficient must
COV(A,B)=   0.0004   be below   0.8438

THE MINIMUM VARIANCE COMBINATION IS   34.00% STOCK A & 66.00% STOCK

                With these proportions, portfolio variance is   0.0007
                               Portfolio standard deviation is   0.0257

                Hit ALT S for a properly scaled graph

PROBLEM 6-10

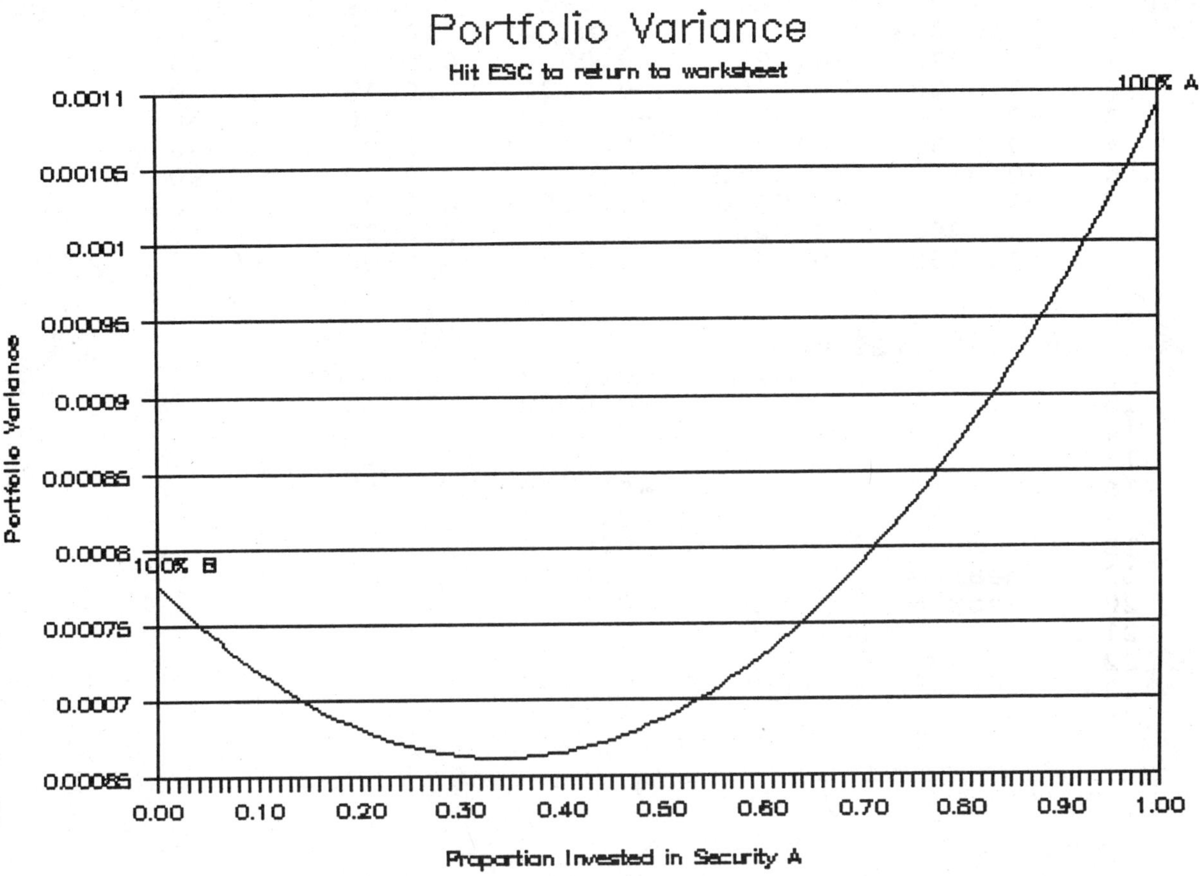
Portfolio Variance
Hit ESC to return to worksheet
100% A
100% B
Portfolio Variance
0.0011
0.00105
0.001
0.00095
0.0009
0.00085
0.0008
0.00075
0.0007
0.00065
0.00
0.10
0.20
0.30
0.40
0.50
0.60
0.70
0.80
0.90
1.00
Proportion Invested in Security A

PROBLEM 6-10

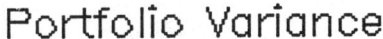

Return #	sec1	sec2	sec3	sec4	sec5 <--input
EXAMPLE	10.00%	-8.00%	20.00%	10.00%	0.00%
1	0.0270	-0.0230	0.0560	0.0020	0.0330
2	0.0120	0.0000	0.0130	0.0040	0.0170
3	-0.0220	-0.0100	-0.0150	0.0020	-0.0450
4	0.0130	0.0340	0.0150	0.0100	0.0080
5	-0.0110	-0.0230	0.0120	-0.0290	-0.0190
6	-0.0330	-0.0610	-0.0350	-0.0220	-0.0240
7	0.0290	0.0260	0.0020	0.0000	-0.0010
8	0.0550	0.0450	0.0470	0.0200	0.0560
9					
10					
11	avg b29..f29 =		0.0190		
12			0.0092		
13			-0.0180		
14			0.0160		
15			-0.0140		
16			-0.0350		
17			0.0112		
18			0.0446		
19	mean =		0.0041		
20	var =		0.0005		
21					
22					
23					
24					

PROBLEM 6-11

Chapter Seven

Why Diversification is a Good Idea

KEY POINTS

This chapter augments chapter six and shows logically (rather than mathematically) why diversification is a good idea. Portfolio risk depends on both the risk of the individual components and their interactions. Portfolio programming seeks to find the least risky way of achieving a particular level of expected return.

Dominance is a central idea introduced here. Investors do not voluntarily accept additional risk unless they expect to be rewarded for doing so. The work of Harry Markowitz is a featured attraction of any portfolio course, and it is covered in this chapter. The development of the efficient frontier is a central idea in portfolio theory.

The Evans and Archer research on naive diversification is arguably one of the most important discoveries in portfolio construction. This should be a central point that all students take away from the course.

The chapter concludes with a discussion of the capital asset pricing model, the estimation of beta via a scattergram, and a brief discussion of the arbitrage pricing theory and its prospects.

TEACHING CONSIDERATIONS

Students must fully understand the idea of dominance after finishing this chapter. Dominance underlies most of finance theory and it should become second nature to those anticipating a career in finance.

It is useful to use the random number generator on Lotus 1-2-3 to show the effects of naive diversification. Prepare five columns of random numbers, and then form two, three, four, and five security equally weighted portfolios. Only bad luck will keep the portfolio variance from declining as the number of securities increases. Do this before class and put the results on a set of overheads. You also can prepare a figure like Figure 7-9 from the data. Everyone should fully understand the implications of the Evans and Archer research and be able to explain why it really isn't necessary for everyone to hold the market portfolio.

It is also a good idea to stress that securities may have a negative expected return and be properly priced, as shown in Figure 7-7. The risk-reduction benefits of negative betas are analogous to the purchase of fire insurance on a house or collision insurance on a car. If the value of a house goes down because of a fire, the value of having the insurance policy goes up. A homeowner does not feel bad at the end of the year if there was no fire and the insurance policy was unused. The same idea holds true with financial assets.

ANSWERS TO QUESTIONS

1. Diversification is a good idea because, properly done, it enables the investor to reduce risk while not sacrificing any expected return. Expected utility is a negative function of risk and a positive function of expected return, so a rational, risk averse investor will always diversify if possible.

2. Your ego can make you reluctant to admit a mistake or cause you to assume a greater degree of risk than you really should.

3. A significant success with a first investment can cause the investor to get cocky and lose perspective on the nature of risk. Too much success early "makes it all seem easy."

4.   Risk that can be diversified away is unnecessary, and the investor is not rewarded for bearing it. Only systematic risk is priced in the market.

5.   Risk from Security A, from Security B, and from the interaction of Securities A and B.

6.   The variance of a well-diversified portfolio is equal to the portfolio's beta squared times the variance of the market.

7.   These securities could be used to lock in a certain return with no risk. Whether this is advantageous or not depends on the alternatives.

8.   They should have the same level of systematic risk.

9.   A gadget costs 34 cents or four for a dollar. No one should ever buy three; the purchase of four dominates the purchase of three.

10.   It shows that it is not necessary to invest in the market portfolio. Very good risk reduction can be achieved with a relatively small portfolio.

11.   Portfolio risk is reduced by selecting securities whose returns are poorly correlated. Securities in the same industry are likely to be highly correlated.

12.   Portfolio theory holds that only systematic risk is rewarded, and beta measures systematic risk.

13.   There may be multiple security portfolios with a lower variance and the same expected return as the single security with the lowest variance. If this is the case, the single security is dominated and does not lie on the efficient frontier.

14.   There is no way to get a higher expected return. Despite its risk, this security is not dominated by any other.

15.   Risk reduction benefits usually accrue anytime a security is added because securities are generally less than perfectly correlated. If, however, the securities have widely different standard deviations, this may not be the case.

16.   Most large institutional investors are precluded from placing more than a certain percentage of their money into

any single security. The lower this percentage, the more securities that must be purchased.

17. It increases.

18. The efficient frontier extends from the riskfree lending rate to the market portfolio, following the curve until it reaches the tangent point to the line extending from the borrowing rate to the efficient frontier for risky assets. The efficient frontier then follows the extension of the borrowing rate line.

19. Naive diversification is unable to guarantee that expected return will be at or above a specified level unless the security universe is carefully selected to include only securities with an expected return of the desired level or greater.

20. They reduce the volume of computer output and show the relative merits of the portfolio components available.

21. Because the standard deviation of a constant is zero and division by zero is not allowed, the correlation between a random variable and a constant is also undefined.

22. The expected return of the market periodically changes as the general level of optimism in the marketplace changes, and as the merits of investment alternatives change (for psychological or other reasons).

23. The CML is measured against variance, while the SML is measured against beta.

24. Beta sometimes changes as the firm's characteristics change (such as its degree of financial leverage) or the risk of its future earnings changes.

25. The market model uses past information to estimate beta, while the CAPM is a theoretical statement about future expected returns.

26. The statement is true. The actual beta is unobservable; empirical evidence is used to estimate it.

27. Availability of data and the ultimate use of the beta. There is some evidence that daily betas contain too much noise and should be avoided.

28.   Normative theories that are developed without a positive underpinning amount to ad hoc theorizing that have very little to do with reality.   Theories should be used to test hypotheses, and hypotheses should originate from observation of actual events, directly or indirectly.

29.   This is a subjective consideration that cannot be globally answered.

30.   The CAPM uses a single "beta" statistic, while the APT uses several.

ANSWERS TO PROBLEMS

1.   a. $E(\tilde{R}_p) = X_A E(\tilde{R}_A) + X_B E(\tilde{R}_B)$

$$= .5(.12) + .5(.13) = .125 = 12.5\%$$

b. $\beta_p = X_A \beta_A + X_B \beta_B$

$$= .5(1.10) + .5(1.20) = 1.15$$

2. $\beta_A = \dfrac{COV(\tilde{A}, \tilde{M})}{\sigma_m^2} = \beta_A \sigma_m^2$

$$= 1.10 \text{ x } .0002 = 2.2 \text{ x } 10^{-4}$$

3. $\sigma_p^2 = X_A^2 \sigma_A^2 + X_B^2 \sigma_B^2 + 2X_A X_B \tau_{AB} \sigma_A \sigma_B$

$$= (.5)^2(.021)^2 + (.5)^2(.029)^2 + 2(.5)(.5)(.6)(.021)(.029)$$

$$= 1.10 \text{ x } 10^{-4} + 2.10 \text{ x } 10^{-4} + 1.83 \text{ x } 10^{-4}$$

$$= 5.03 \text{ x } 10^{-4}$$

$$\dfrac{1.83 \text{ x } 10^{-4}}{5.03 \text{ x } 10^{-4}} = 36.4\%$$

4. $5.03 \text{ x } 10^{-4}$

5. $\sigma_p^2 = X_A^2 \sigma_A^2 + X_B^2 \sigma_B^2 + X_C^2 \sigma_C^2 + X_A X_C \tau_{AC} \sigma_A \sigma_C + X_A X_B \tau_{AB} \sigma_A \sigma_B +$

$$X_B X_C \tau_{BC} \sigma_B \sigma_C$$

$$\min \sigma_p^2$$

subject to

$$X_A + X_B + X_C = 1.0$$

$$X_A, X_B, X_C \geq 0 \text{ (optional)}$$

6. $E(\check{R}) = X_A \, E(\check{R}_A) + X_B \, E(\check{R}_B)$

$$= .5(8\%) + .5(13\%) = 10.5\%$$

$$\sigma_p^2 = X_A^2 \sigma_A^2 + X_B \sigma_B^2 + 2X_A X_B \tau_{AB} \sigma_A \sigma_B$$

$$= \quad 0 \quad + X_B \sigma_B^2 + \quad 0$$

$$= (.5)^2 \ \sigma_B^2 = .25(.029)^2 = 2.10 \times 10^{-4}$$

7. Omitted.

8. See attached page.

9. See attached page.

10. From Chapter 6:

$$\text{min variance } X_A = \frac{\sigma_B^2 - \sigma_A \sigma_B \tau_{AB}}{\sigma_A^2 + \sigma_B^2 - 2\sigma_A \sigma_B \tau_{AB}}$$

$\sigma_A, \ \sigma_B > 0$ if $\tau_{AB} < 1$

for $X_B = 0, \ X_A = 1$

If this is true,

$$\sigma_A^2 + \sigma_B^2 - 2\sigma_A \sigma_B \tau_{AB} = \sigma_B^2 - \sigma_A \sigma_B \tau_{AB}$$

$$\sigma_A^2 - 2\sigma_A \sigma_B \tau_{AB} = - \sigma_A \sigma_B \tau_{AB}$$

$$\sigma_A^2 - \sigma_A \sigma_B \tau_{AB} = 0$$

$$\sigma_A^2 = \sigma_A \sigma_B \tau_{AB}$$

$\sigma_A = \sigma_B \tau_{AB}$ which is possible

therefore the statement is true.

DETERMINING THE MINIMUM VARIANCE
TWO-SECURITY PORTFOLIO

Enter the appropriate information in column C:

Variance of Stock A: 0.0002   (Standard deviation = 0.0136)

Variance of Stock B: 0.0004   (Standard deviation = 0.0195)

Correlation between   For diversification benefits,
Stocks A and B: -0.6050   the correlation coefficient must
COV(A,B)= -0.0002   be below 0.6977

THE MINIMUM VARIANCE COMBINATION IS   61.01% STOCK A &   38.99% STOCK B

       With these proportions, portfolio variance is   0.0001
                        Portfolio standard deviation is   0.0071

              Hit ALT S for a properly scaled graph

PROBLEM 7-8

DETERMINING THE MINIMUM VARIANCE
TWO-SECURITY PORTFOLIO

Enter the appropriate information in column C:

Variance of Stock A: 0.0002   (Standard deviation = 0.0136)

Variance of Stock B: 0.0003   (Standard deviation = 0.0176)

Correlation between   For diversification benefits,
Stocks A and B: -0.6050   the correlation coefficient must
COV(A,B)= -0.0001   be below 0.7725

THE MINIMUM VARIANCE COMBINATION IS   57.96% STOCK A &   42.04% STOCK B

        With these proportions, portfolio variance is   .0000
                      Portfolio standard deviation is   0.0068

            Hit ALT S for a properly scaled graph

PROBLEM 7-9

11. Omitted.

12. (1) Form a portfolio of 50% SEC1 and 50% SEC2.   Its beta
         is 1.10 and its expected return is 11%.

     (2) Buy SEC3 [β=1.10, $E(\check{R})$=13%]

     (3) Sell short the SEC1/SEC2 portfolio

     β_p = 0, $E(\check{R})$ = 2%

13. σ_p = $(.26)^{.5}$ = .5099

     σ_{xxz} = $(.20)^{.5}$ = .4472

     $$\frac{.4472}{.5099} = .8771 \qquad \tau < .8771; \text{ therefore, YES.}$$

14. See attached

15. Omitted.

16. See attached.

17. $E(\check{R})$ = R_f + $\beta E[\check{R}_m - R_f]$

             = .08 + 1.23[.14 - .08] = 15.38%

18. 14% = .07 + 1.00[$E(\check{R}_m)$ - .07]

         ==> $E(\check{R}_m)$ = 14%

     $E(\check{R})$ = .07 + 2.00[.14 - .07] = 21%

19. See attached.

20. Omitted.

21. True β = 0.9833 +/- 2(.3354)

              .3125 $\leq \beta \leq$ 1.6541

     The beta estimate is not very reliable.

22. 1.22 +/- 2(.04)   1.14 $\leq \beta \leq$ 1.30

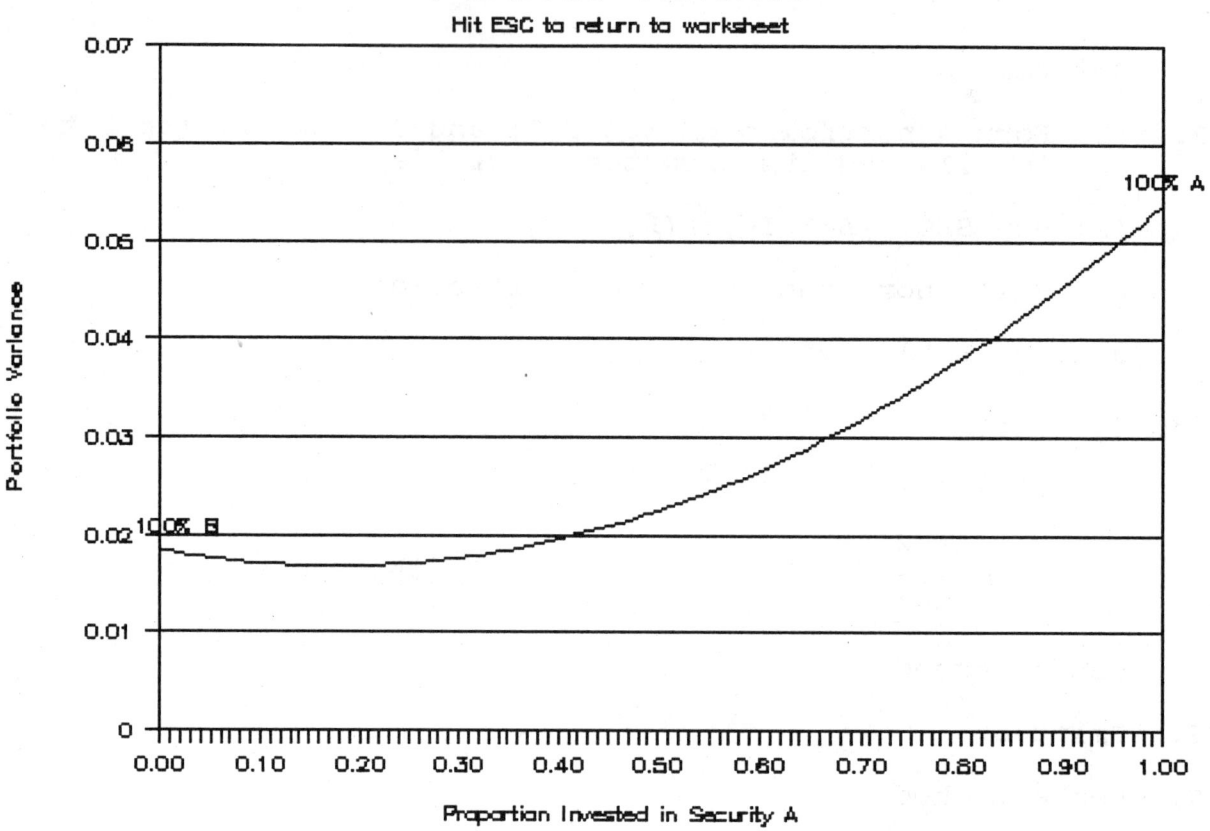

PROBLEM 7-14a

DETERMINING THE MINIMUM VARIANCE
TWO-SECURITY PORTFOLIO

Enter the appropriate information in column C:

Variance of Stock A: 0.0005   (Standard deviation = 0.0232)

Variance of Stock B: 0.0002   (Standard deviation = 0.0136)

Correlation between   For diversification benefits,
Stocks A and B: 0.2860   the correlation coefficient must
COV(A,B)=   0.0001   be below   0.5864

THE MINIMUM VARIANCE COMBINATION IS   17.47% STOCK A &   82.53% STOCK B

      With these proportions, portfolio variance is   0.0002
                          Portfolio standard deviation is   0.0130

            Hit ALT S for a properly scaled graph

PROBLEM 7-14b

Problem 7-16

		Regression Output:	
0.06	0.08		
-0.02	0	Constant	-0.00298
-0.03	-0.04	Std Err of Y Est	0.007314
0	0.01	R Squared	0.950234
0.01	0.01	No. of Observations	10
0.04	0.05	Degrees of Freedom	8
-0.01	-0.01		
0.03	0.04	X Coefficient(s) 0.763740	
-0.02	-0.03	Std Err of Coef. 0.061794	
0.04	0.06		

Problem 7-19a

		Regression Output:	
0.06	0.08		
-0.02	0	Constant	-0.00540
-0.03	-0.04	Std Err of Y Est	0.010474
0	0.01	R Squared	0.933100
0.01	0.01	No. of Observations	5
		Degrees of Freedom	3
		X Coefficient(s) 0.783422	
		Std Err of Coef. 0.121110	

Problem 7-19b

		Regression Output:	
0.04	0.05		
-0.01	-0.01	Constant	0.000095
0.03	0.04	Std Err of Y Est	0.003554
-0.02	-0.03	R Squared	0.988584
0.04	0.06	No. of Observations	5
		Degrees of Freedom	3
		X Coefficient(s) 0.722929	
		Std Err of Coef. 0.044850	

Chapter Eight

The Capital Markets and Market Efficiency

KEY POINTS

The U. S. capital markets are the envy of much of the rest
of the industrialized world. Their three functions are a
good introduction to the notion of market efficiency. When
we speak of market efficiency, we refer to _informational_
efficiency (the rapid adjustment of prices to new information) rather than _operational_ efficiency (the extent to which
orders get lost or improperly filled).

There are three forms to market efficiency, with the semi-
efficient market hypothesis being a useful cousin to the
traditional paradigm. There is a difference between the
random walk theory and the efficient market hypothesis.
Anomalies remain a puzzle and are a continuing area of financial research.

TEACHING CONSIDERATIONS

Remind students of the distinction between the capital
market and the money market. The former is a physical place
where long-term securities (like common stock and bonds) are
traded, while the latter is an electronic linkup of the
largest commercial banks where short-term securities (like
treasury bills) are traded.

Students are quite interested in the business of charting
and technical analysis in general. While this text does not
cover much of this subject, many instructors will want to

53

digress into this area a bit. A coin flipping exercise to build a chart on the chalkboard followed by a test of the randomness of the pattern via a runs test is always useful and seemingly interesting to the class. I assign a homework problem using the RUNS file from the Strong Software disk.

Stress the fact that market efficiency does not mean that no one can make a profit in the stock market. It means that because the news cannot be consistently anticipated, long-term rates of return will be consistent with their associated level of risk.

Anomalies are another topic of interest to most students. There are certain things in finance that we do not know, and this fact should be clearly shown to the class. Fibonacci numbers are an example of pure market folklore, but a fascinating subject (with most university libraries subscribing to the highly mathematical <u>Fibonacci</u> <u>Quarterly</u>).

ANSWERS TO QUESTIONS

1. It is still necessary to gather security statistics (such as betas and covariances) for portfolio construction purposes, and it is also the activities of security analysts that, to a large extent, help keep the market efficient.

2. This is a common, and very dangerous, question. Security markets are quite efficient, but they are not completely efficient. The logic of the semi-efficient market hypothesis is compelling, and there is the issue of the anomalies.

3. Only the name is similar. The semi-efficient market hypothesis deals with the existence of different "tiers" of stocks with differing levels of investor interest, while the semi-strong form deals with the extent of the information set.

4. Market efficiency means that security prices adjust quickly and accurately to news; the random walk theory states that the news arrives randomly, so security price changes cannot be predicted.

5. Do students tend to arrive in the classroom in groups of the same sex?

6. The weak form of the EMH holds that the current stock price fully reflects any information contained in the past price series. If this is true, charts cannot be used to

predict the future.

7. Informational efficiency deals with the accuracy and speed with which security prices react to arriving information; operational efficiency deals with the accuracy and speed at which orders are processed.

8. Continuous pricing refers to the fact that the current value of a security can be readily determined from the financial pages or from a computer terminal. Fair pricing refers to the end result of market efficiency: over the long term, security prices reflect their proper expected return given their level of risk.

9. The evidence suggests that charting does not work. The problem is that most chartists are unable to define precisely the charting techniques they use and the associated decision rules. Also, there is much that we do not know about finance, and it is likely that the supply and demand dimensions of charting may contain some information that we do not know how to unearth.

10. A positive intercept does not necessarily mean the market is inefficient. It may mean that the model generating the intercept is misspecified, that the market index is incorrect, or that the result is time period specific.

11. A true test of market efficiency should determine whether any apparent abnormal profits are actually realizable. If you must pay a dollar to get a "free" fifty cents, it is not clear that an inefficiency really exists.

12. There is much folklore about the price/earnings ratio. The traditional PE is related to past earnings, while it is future earnings that matter most. There is no consensus on what constitutes a good PE, although the empirical evidence is slightly on the side of low PEs.

13. Many people believe that low stock prices are positively correlated with the level of risk: low priced stocks are risky.

14. If small firms do generate larger returns than expected by finance theory, it would make sense for portfolios to concentrate on firms with low capitalization.

ANSWERS TO PROBLEMS

1.   See attached page.

2.   Omitted.

3.   Omitted.

4.   Omitted.

5.   Omitted.

RUNS TEST

Input R, N1, and N2 below:

A run is an uninterrupted series of the same sign. For instance, the series below has 6 runs:

# of runs (R):   8
N1:   10
N2:   5
mean: 7.67
sigma: 1.64

Z score: 0.20

```
H  H  H  T  T  H  T  H  T  T  T
^           ^     ^  ^  ^     ^
|           |     |  |  |     |
1           2     3  4  5     6
```

R=6, N1=5, N2=6
(or R=6, N1=6, N2=5)

PROBABILITY OF   8 RUNS OUT OF   15 OBSERVATIONS
OCCURING BY CHANCE: 41.96%

(This test is best used when N1 and N2 both exceed 20.)

PROBLEM 8-1

Chapter Nine

International Investment and Diversification

KEY POINTS

Diversifying internationally makes sense because the evidence shows that the level of risk in a portfolio can be reduced by doing so. Replication of the Evans and Archers study results in a lower level of undiversifiable risk when the security universe includes international securities.

Because foreign securities are denominated in a currency other than dollars, the international investor faces foreign exchange risk: there is a chance of loss due to changing currency values. Foreign exchange rates are partially determined by relative interest rates and inflation rates among the world's countries.

The extent to which someone faces foreign exchange risk is called exposure. Exposure can be hedged via the futures market, the forward market, or the options market.

Political risk is another dimension of risk that concerns the international investor. It stems from changes in the political environment in which a firm conducts its business.

While it is possible to invest directly in foreign securities, many investors find the purchase of ADRs or international mutual funds a simpler alternative.

TEACHING CONSIDERATIONS

Not all students will be able to take a course in international business or international finance. This chapter covers several principal topics contained in such a course.

From a portfolio perspective, the main teaching point here is the diversification benefit which empirical research shows is available through the addition of foreign securities to a portfolio. From an "education of the business student" perspective, the new sources of risk (foreign exchange and political) are key points.

ANSWERS TO QUESTIONS

1. Ideally, the decision to invest internationally is based on some analytics. In practice, the decision is usually a subjective one based on qualitative rather than quantitative factors. Some firms, though, do view international securities as a separate asset class. If this is the case, it is not clear the concept of superfluous diversification is relevant.

2. Many world exchanges have fewer securities and fewer industry effects. This means the existing securities tend to move together, or that a given security contributes heavily to the total "market" performance.

3. Capital constraints keep many people from diversifying properly. Mutual funds could be used for this purpose, but some people feel they are "not exciting." It is likely that many people are unfamiliar with the ease with which many foreign securities can be acquired.

4. When all the players are of equal caliber, there may be some truth to this statement. Often, however, the U. S. dollar rises or falls against most of the rest of the world currencies simultaneously.

5. A succession of short-term hedges is usually more expensive than a single long-term hedge. You do have more flexibility in a sense, but you pay for it.

6. An increase in inflation results in an upward adjustment in the level of interest rates. If both countries experience an equal increase in inflation and everything else remains constant, it is likely that the relative exchange rate would not change.

7. Economic exposure results in an actual dollar change in the performance of an investment. Accounting exposure is of concern to a multinational corporation that must prepare consolidated financial statements.

8. Yes. Congress could easily change the rules regarding tariffs, withholding taxes, or tax credits.

9. Political risk is sometimes partially insurable through an insurance company. It generally cannot be hedged with a normal financial instrument.

10. Financial investment, as this is associated with securities.

11. Investor A, because the greatest diversification benefits occur with the early additions to a portfolio.

12. Probably micro risk.

13. ADRs enable you to trade foreign securities on a U. S. exchange quickly through a U. S. brokerage firm.

14. First check the Weissenberger's and Morningstar services to see if it happened to be listed. You also could check the Wall Street Journal index. If you had no luck here the best bet, frankly, is to ask for help from your local reference librarian. Most libraries have some information regarding foreign securities.

15. The currency forward market is not designed as a speculative arena. Forward contracts are purely hedging devices. You do not expect to "make money" in them.

16. They could easily be included in the equity portion.

17. Some type of goal programming, regression, or linear programming model could be used to identify securities that meet certain criteria or offer the "best" package of predetermined characteristics. A business climate index, being a numerical measure, could easily be incorporated.

18. Yes. Changes in relative foreign exchange rates will still affect the value of the security underlying the ADR.

19. Some Wall Street firms are currently advertising international fixed income products, but it is not immediately

obvious what role these have in a diversification sense.

ANSWERS TO PROBLEMS

1. $1.00 = G1.4456   ==> $0.6918/G   Spot

US T bill = 8.68%

60 day forward rate = $0.7100/G

$$\text{Forward premium} = \frac{\text{spot} - \text{forward}}{\text{forward}} \times \frac{12}{N} \times 100$$

= -15.38% (discount)

therefore, G interest rate = US rate - discount

= 8.68% - (-15.38%) = 24.06%

2.   Omitted.

3.   Omitted.

4.   C$1.00 = $0.75

1% inflation in US ==> US $ will depreciate by 1%

C$1.00 = $0.75(1.01) = $0.7575 ==> $0.76

5.   Omitted.

6.   There are SFr 125,000 in one futures contract.

     a.   In the forward market, sell the principal (and last interest check, if desired) forward for delivery in 90 days.

     b.   With futures, sell $\dfrac{\text{SFr 1 million}}{\text{SFr 125,000/contract}}$ = 8 contracts

7.   Buy SFr puts (SFr 62,500 per contract)

     ==> $\dfrac{10 \text{ million}}{62,500}$ = 160 contracts

     or write deep-in-the-money calls (or do both)

8. forward premium $= \dfrac{¥136.15 - ¥135.90}{¥135.90} \times \dfrac{12}{6} \times 100 = 0.37\%$

If the Japanese rate is 8%, the US rate should be

8.00% - 0.37% = 7.63%

So the markets are not in equilibrium.

Chapter Ten

Picking the Equity Players

There are three key teaching points in this chapter:

1. The types of dividends and their payment procedure;
2. Why dividends and stock prices may be neutral events rather than windfall gains;
3. Categories of common stock.

TEACHING CONSIDERATIONS

As an instructor, I find coverage of this material especially enjoyable. This material is mostly "investments" material, and some students will have previously encountered these ideas and key points. Still, the review is always worthwhile.

I highly recommend the "shoebox example." The notion that dividends do not come out of the sky, and that they are really a neutral occurrence at best, is both disturbing and fascinating to many people. I find that the shoebox example is one thing that students remember the longest from their study of the market.

Stress the importance of the ex-dividend date and the fact that it is a brokerage industry tradition rather than being announced by the company. The ex-dividend date convention arose because of investors' dislike of the uncertainty surrounding mail times, clerical screw-ups, and whether they would get the forthcoming dividend. To deal with this, the

brokerage industry established the uniform policy of establishing an inviolable cut-off point four business days before
the date of record.

A good analogy of the neutral nature of stock splits and
stock dividends is with the size of pizza slices. You cannot
increase the quantity of pizza merely by cutting the pie into
more slices. The same thing is true of the value of a firm.

ANSWERS TO QUESTIONS

1. The value of a firm is determined by its assets and its
liabilities. You cannot increase the value of the firm by
increasing the number of ownership pieces into which it is
cut.

2. Stock dividends are "cheaper" than cash dividends, in
that their only cost is clerical and administrative. Cash
dividends require a cash outlay in addition. There is some
psychological advantage to a stock dividend over no dividend,
and if this is the case stock dividends may have merit.

3. There is little empirical data on property dividends.
The same principles, however, should hold. Giving away
company assets should reduce the value of a share.

4. Changes in dividend policy are widely believed to have a
signaling function. When dividends are different from what
analysts expect, the market invariably tries to read something into the unexpected event. To this extent, the statement has merit.

5. You could look at a plot of the stock price relative to
some macroeconomic measure related to the total economy such
as GNP or housing starts.

6. This is true. An investor is interested in total return.
If no dividends are paid, the stock price must advance in
order for the stock to generate a return. Funds which are
paid out cannot be reinvested in the firm to earn an additional return, but they can be invested by the investor. The
classic investment "dog stock" is one with no dividends whose
price does not change.

7. The value of a share of stock comes from its being a
claim on the assets (and future earnings power) of the firm.
The firm presumably has some value, and the owner of the firm

could realize this value by selling all the shares.   The shares, therefore, must have value or arbitrage would be present.

8.   Both securities will decline unless the information was completely anticipated by the market.   Because the preferred stock carries a claim on omitted dividends, its value is likely to increase (everything else being equal) as time passes.

9.   Negative changes in dividend policy are interpreted as bad signals in the marketplace.   The firm seeks to maximize shareholder wealth, and management may feel that payment of the dividend is the lesser of two evils.

10.   A reduction in the discount rate corresponds to a reduction in risk.   This means that the valuation equation for the security has a smaller number in the denominator, and therefore the present value of the anticipated cash flow stream increases.   This increases the market value of the security.

11.   The ticketholder can 1) use the ticket (exercise the option), 2) sell the ticket (sell the rights), or 3) abandon the tickets and not go to the game (let the rights expire).

12.   The board of directors seeks to maximize the aggregate value of the company's shares.   The price of an individual share does not matter; the total value of all the shares does.

ANSWERS TO PROBLEMS

1.   1000 x 1.10 x 1.20 x 1.25 x 2 x 2 x 2 = 13,200

2.   Omitted.

3.   Omitted.

4.   GE -- General Electric
     SWV -- Suave Shoe
     MHS -- Marriott Corporation
     P -- Phillips Petroleum
     DBRSY -- DeBeers Consolidated Mines ADR

5. a. $4,165,212 - $100 = $4,165,112

    b.   This is a good example of the accounting concept of materiality.   It would be difficult to determine the answer to this question precisely, but the precise answer is immaterial. The current value is over $4 million and the cost basis is only $100. For all practical purposes, the entire current value is a capital gain.

6. Omitted.

7. Calculate g:

If originally you owned 1 share, now you have 4. Current dividends are then $0.16 x 4 = $0.64.

$$.30(1 + g)^{10} = .64$$

$$g = (.64/.30)^{.1} - 1 = 7.87\%$$

$$PV = \frac{\$0.16(1.0787)}{.14 - .0787} = \$2.82$$

8. Omitted.

9. PV = $8

a. g_1 = infinite

b. $.10(1 + g)^3 = .18$ g = 21.6%

10 - 18.   Omitted.

Chapter Eleven

Bond Selection

KEY POINTS

Bond selection is a topic that often receives only minimal coverage in both textbooks and literature from the trade. Bonds are important components of many portfolios, and the selection of them should be by design.

With bonds, the investor is concerned with default risk and with interest rate risk. Reinvestment rate risk is a secondary concern, but still an important one. As expected, there is a trade-off between yield and maturity. What constitutes an adequate additional expected return for additional risk is a moot point about which investment managers probably will never reach consensus.

It can be a considerable inconvenience if a bond is called, particularly if the bond appears in many managed portfolios. This is an example of a convenience risk.

The "monthly retirement income" example is the meat of this chapter and considerable time should be spent on it. Finance students often complain that they don't know how to "do anything," and building such a bond portfolio is something they clearly can do right away. People routinely hire brokers and financial advisors to do this for them.

TEACHING CONSIDERATIONS

Be sure to incorporate the BONDPORT file from the Strong Software disk in the coverage of this material. I assign a homework assignment using this file. [Note: there is an occasional error arising with the BONDPORT file. Interest payment months must be entered in chronological order. For instance, a bond that pays interest in February and August must be entered with the "f" first, followed by the "a." As the file instructions indicate, letters can be either upper or lower case.]

I like to use a handout from the Standard & Poor's Bond Guide to augment classroom discussion. This enables you to reinforce the notion of different interest payment months and consider the higher yields associated with lower bond ratings. You also can construct a monthly income schedule (or at least part of one) as with the BONDPORT file.

ANSWERS TO QUESTIONS

1. A primary objective of income means that the generation of income is paramount. Therefore, the current yield (which is a direct function of the coupon rate) is more important than yield to maturity.

2. Yes. Bonds with identical durations generally have the same yield to maturity unless they have very different liquidity risk or other characteristics.

3. 1) Interest rates in the economy fell; 2) it sells at a discount and has moved closer to maturity; 3) the bond rating was increased; 4) it is a convertible bond and the stock price increased.

4. When bonds sell for a premium, it is because their coupon rate is higher than average, so investors are willing to pay more for it. The yield to maturity is the factor that matters long term. Some people, however, do not understand why you would buy something that you know will go down in value. The fact that the income received compensates for this can be overlooked. Some managers prefer to avoid having to explain this fact of life.

5. It is an inconvenience having a bond called. Some people avoid buying a callable bond because they want to avoid having to deal with replacement decisions or the effort involved in doing so.

6.   You can lose money if the call price is less than the price you paid.

7.   There is no clear-cut answer to this one.   Experience and personal opinion are very relevant.

8.   Many people would say no.   Still, it is never a good idea to buy any security without knowing a good deal about the issuer.

9.   See the equation in footnote 3.   Beta is directly related to the negative of duration.

10.   They sometimes have a slightly higher yield to maturity than otherwise similar bonds selling at par or at a discount.

11.   Investors value the conversion option.   They essentially buy a call option on the stock, and the premium on the option takes the form of a reduced yield.

12.   This depends on the covariance between the change in market interest rates and the return on the market index. Often when interest rates rise, the stock market falls.   If this is the case, the beta will be negative.

13.   Probably not.   You cannot have your cake and eat it, too, so the rate at which funds would be reinvested is not a concern.

ANSWERS TO PROBLEMS

1.   Omitted.

2.   Omitted.

3.   Cost = principal + interest + commission

$$= (.99 \times \$5000) + (\$5000 \times .1025 \times 73/365) + \$40$$

$$= \$4950 + 102.50 + 40 = \$5092.50$$

4. $\$500,000 \times .085 \times 1/4 = \$10,625$

5 - 11.   Omitted.

Chapter Twelve

Security Screening

KEY POINTS

Every investor engages in some form of security screening. Despite this, few books devote much space to the topic. This chapter shows how a logical screen can be developed and how it can help the investor narrow the potential choices.

Very good screens can be developed using only the financial press. More sophisticated screens are available through published investment advisory services (such as Value Line) or via the computer (such as StockPak II).

TEACHING CONSIDERATIONS

To most people, the logic of screening is obvious. Where students need reassurance is in their developing self confidence regarding their ability to carry out a screen they design on their own. As long as a screen satisfies the three basic criteria described in the chapter, it is a valid tool. Stress that there is no right way to screen; specific techniques used are a matter of personal preference.

You should make good use of Value Line handouts. Show how the service provides ready-made screens via its various sections (as shown in the chapter). Consider incorporating Value Line into a portfolio construction problem using PORT-MAN.

ANSWERS TO QUESTIONS

1. If earnings are negative, some people would consider this to be a disqualifying security characteristic.

2. The firm probably has no debt.

3. Criteria that could be used include high school class rank, grade point average, national merit scholar status, member of the national honor society, and club activities and sport participation.

4. A high dividend yield is often due to a decline in the stock price. The dividend yield is usually high right before the dividend is discontinued, too.

5. Phillips or flat head; industrial, household, or jeweler size.

6. There is "no accounting for taste." It is hard to say that a subjective screening criterion is inappropriate if it makes sense to the user. Good alternatives may be eliminated, but that is often the case with any screening technique.

7. There is mixed evidence about this, although the empirical evidence slightly favors the low-PE approach.

8. Many people would consider this to be a risky stock because of its "low" stock price.

9. You need to relax one or more of the screens. It is likely that the criteria are not all equally important, and the least important criterion should be the first to go.

10. It is likely that the higher the beta, the higher the variance of ROE.

11. No.

12. No.

ANSWERS TO PROBLEMS

1. Price; power vs manual; riding vs non-riding; if non-riding, power propelled vs pushed; width of cut; brand recognition.

2 - 7.   omitted

8.   Taco Bell --> Pepsico
     Frito Lay --> Pepsico
     Wilson Sporting Goods --> Pepsico
     Burger King --> Grand Metropolitan PLC

9.   Stock symbols: BEP, BZ, BEZ, BLY, BFL, BKB, B, BAX, BGC, BER, BI, BRY, BKH, BAW

Chapter Thirteen

The Role of Real Assets

KEY POINTS

   Modern investment decisions involve more than just stocks
and bonds. Pension funds are rapidly discovering the role
that "non-traditional" assets like gold and timberland can
play in their portfolios.

   This chapter provides a brief introduction to real estate,
with a focus on timberland, as this is a little-known but
increasingly important pension fund asset.

TEACHING CONSIDERATIONS

   The trade publication <u>Pensions</u> <u>and</u> <u>Investments</u> has an
article about timberland on a very regular basis. As with
many developments in finance (such as futures and options
usage), the broader market is sometimes slow to get the word.
Pension funds have known about timberland for years, yet the
individual investor is usually surprised to learn that institutions hold this asset in such quantity.

   As the chapter shows, this material is intended as a
primer on the basic principles of timberland investment. The
notion of product class shift (Figure 13-3) is an often-
overlooked aspect of a forest. While there is a continuing
problem with a lack of a consistent timberland index, the
evidence is clear regarding timberland's general tendency to
move counter to the stock market, thereby providing significant portfolio diversification benefits.

Point out the fact that the whole idea of the time value of money actually began in the forestry literature. Note the Faustmann reference after chapter two.

Gold is a better-known asset than timberland, and in some respects just as important. There are various ways to invest in gold, ranging from actual securities to bullion bars. Many institutions who choose to hold gold do so because of a belief that gold is an inflation hedge or because of a perceived tendency for gold to move counter to the equity markets and provide diversification benefits.

There is an excellent videotape available from the National Geographic Society entitled simply "Gold." This hour-long production is a very good overview of the pricing, mining, and heritage of gold.

ANSWERS TO QUESTIONS

1. A financial asset has a corresponding liability; a real asset does not, although one might be produced to finance the asset.

2. Developed land is better suited to generating income than undeveloped land. Most investors buy undeveloped land with the intent of selling it later at a profit.

3. Real estate is the tangible asset; real property is a legal interest in real estate.

4. Residential, commercial, industrial, farm, special purpose

5. All land areas are unique; even adjacent plots will differ concerning their microsite factors. This means they are not all equally desirable, and therefore not equally valuable.

6. As collateral, as a strategic investment, as a pure investment.

7. Volume of wood, diameter of the trees, market price of the species.

8. Timber prices, land values, product class shifts, biological growth.

9. Biological risks deal with the possibility of loss from a natural event such as fire, wind, disease, or insects. Economic risks deal with liquidity, regulatory, or management issues.

10. Such an index probably should be based on both the market value of a species of timber and a reflection of the usual timber growth rate. It is likely that more than one index will always be necessary to provide complete information about timber prices.

11. No. Poor management can adversely affect the value of just about anything.

12. Larger trees are worth much more than smaller trees. As the diameter of a tree passes through certain thresholds, the tree becomes suited for more expensive purposes. Forests which are undergoing a product class shift are more valuable than younger forests.

13. Such an index ignores the fact that trees act as their own factory. This means that there will be an increase in the value of the wood even if the market price remains constant.

14. Relative value of world currencies, anticipated inflation and its impact on oil prices, world uncertainty, extraordinary demand (such as the Japanese gold coin phenomenon), and the London fix.

15. Bullion, gold shares, gold certificates, gold coins

16. A twice-daily settlement price for gold determined by a group of British banks. The London fix seeks to find an equilibrium price balancing supply and demand.

17. The "European cartel" refers to the London fix, and this is not really a cartel. Also, the London fixing procedure probably would not be able to manipulate the market price of gold beyond the equilibrium value for very long.

18. Many pension funds have begun to include managed futures in their portfolios for precisely this reason.

Chapter Fourteen

Revision of the Equity Portfolio

KEY POINTS

An important point in this chapter is the distinction between active and passive management. While there is nothing wrong with a naive buy-and-hold strategy with common stock, many investors choose to actively manage their portfolio by periodically changing the components.

Portfolios can be rebalanced in various ways. The constant beta and constant proportion methods illustrate two common ways in which this might be done.

Some people find the decision when to sell stock to be at least as difficult as the decision regarding what stock to buy in the first place. Crawling stop orders can be very helpful in coordinating the sale with a previously established target sales price.

Dollar cost averaging is a valuable investment technique for the individual. It is covered in the portfolio memo.

TEACHING CONSIDERATIONS

Use overheads to walk through the events surrounding Tables 14-1 through 14-5. Review the importance of commissions and managerial time constraints associated with frequent rebalancing, as well as the possibility of being accused of churning.

Be sure to go through the dollar cost averaging portfolio memo. The notion that a fluctuating portfolio whose value begins and ends at the same price can earn more than a steadily rising portfolio is surprising, but true.

Finally, make up an example of an investor who buys a stock and has a target price in mind at which it will be sold. Show how a crawling stop can be used to protect profits but leave open the possibility of future price appreciation on the stock. If the stock is sold, the claim to future appreciation is lost.

ANSWERS TO QUESTIONS

1.   There is much to be said in favor of buy-and-hold strategies. Ideally, though, such a strategy is used on purpose rather than because of inattention. To the extent that most portfolios require the periodic reinvestment of dividend and interest income received, the statement is true: the portfolio will routinely be revised as cash accumulates. The portfolio also will periodically encounter mergers, tender offers, and rights offerings, and these also have portfolio revision overtones.

2.   Someone who rebalances wants to maintain a portfolio with particular investment characteristics. Whether these characteristics are reasonable or not is another story. The empirical evidence also suggests that managers are not able consistently to time the market or earn a return greater than that associated with the security's level of risk. In some respects, an active manager does not believe in the efficient market hypothesis.

3.   Commissions must be paid, there may be tax considerations, and it takes time.

4.   A crawling stop provides protection (although incomplete protection in the event of a crash; a stop order activates a market order, and the market price may change quickly) against adverse price movements while leaving open the possibility of further gains. The stop price can be moved behind a rising stock to protect a progressively larger profit.

5.   Ignorance is the primary reason, and stockbrokers seem to forget to recommend them to their customers.

6.   A correlation of .96 is very high. To move closer to 1.00 would be expensive in terms of additional commissions,

and probably is not necessary. Still, on a large portfolio, a failure to mimic the market as best as possible might result in unacceptably large deviations in the dollar value of the portfolio from the target value.

7. If a portfolio states its objective as capital apprecia- tion, it should normally be an equity portfolio. A mutual fund with such an objective probably would not be able to convert completely to cash because of prospectus provisions. Market risk could, however, be reduced via derivative assets such as stock index futures or options.

8. Probably not, although some people might feel that 15% is too far away from the current price.

9. This is a moot point that is routinely argued in courts of law. An important factor is the manager's performance; did the unusually high level of turnover result in gains to the customer or only commissions in the broker's pocket?

10. This is a restrictive constraint. A portfolio might be equally weighted or constant beta, but doing both is more technical. It can be done, but might be expensive in terms of the number of adjustments required.

11. Most portfolios generate cash. As the level of cash held increases, the portfolio beta declines because cash has a beta of zero and will "water down" the risk of the portfo- lio.

12. Security prices will fluctuate. If the market is effi- cient, though, they will show an appropriate expected return over long term. This means that they should be bought in a period when they perform poorer than their expected return, as they will (on average) make it up in a subsequent period. The converse holds true if they do unusually well.

ANSWERS TO PROBLEMS

1. Omitted

2. The basic approach is to sell some stocks that have appreciated and buy more of those that have declined.

3. Using the SPECULATIVE PORTFOLIO option and set the mini- mum investment equal to the market value of each stock. This results in a portfolio beta of 1.08.

4.   Cash has a beta of zero. Therefore, selling a proportional amount of every portfolio asset and holding the proceeds in cash will reduce the beta proportionately, too. Solve for X in the following ratio:

$$\frac{250000}{1.10} = \frac{250000 - X}{0.95}$$

X = 34901

Sell $34,091 in stock.

5. This is a market rise of (360.25 - 340.15)/340.15 = 5.9%. Each security should therefore rise by its beta multiplied by 5.9%:

$$
\begin{array}{lccc}
\text{JUI:} & 1.07 \times 5.9\% & = & 6.31\% \\
\text{LLO:} & 0.92 \times 5.9\% & = & 5.43\% \\
\text{KI:} & 1.10 \times 5.9\% & = & 6.49\% \\
\text{NMB:} & 1.22 \times 5.9\% & = & 7.20\% \\
\text{ERW:} & 1.10 \times 5.9\% & = & 6.49\% \\
\text{OP:} & 0.88 \times 5.9\% & = & 5.19\% \\
\text{XXC:} & 1.00 \times 5.9\% & = & 5.90\% \\
\text{PPM:} & 1.03 \times 5.9\% & = & 6.08\% \\
\text{PPU:} & 1.22 \times 5.9\% & = & 7.20\% \\
\text{WQE:} & 1.14 \times 5.9\% & = & 6.73\% \\
\end{array}
$$

6.   Final portfolio:

Company	Weight	Price	Shrs	Value	
YH	10%	90	133	11970	(sell 67)
POE	10%	126	95	11970	(sell 5)
LOL	10%	13	919	11947	(buy 119)
FC	10%	20	597	11940	(buy 197)
HG	10%	15	796	11940	(buy 96)
QWS	10%	30	398	11940	(sell 102)
ZR	10%	60	199	11940	(sell 51)
LO	10%	55	217	11935	(buy 67)
EDT	10%	27	442	11934	(buy 142)
GTY	10%	80	149	11920	(sell 1)

Cash = $564   (use $1,586)

Total Portfolio Value
$120000

7. $\sigma^2_m = .04$ $\beta = 1.05$ $\sigma^2_p = ?$

from equation 6-9a, $\sigma^2_p = \beta^2_p \sigma^2_p$

$$= 1.05 \times .04 = 0.042$$

8. a) Variance of A = 0.001660   Variance of B = 0.000910
(Note that the variance is of the returns, not of the share
price.)

    b) At the end of the period, 121.218 shares would have
been accumulated in Fund A. Worth $12.76 apiece, this is a
total value of $1,546.74. In Fund B, 122.17 shares would
have been accumulated. At $13.08 apiece, this fund value is
$1,597.98.

9. A good teaching point is raised in this question. Con-
tributions were made into the funds; if these are not considered, the apparent fund return will be substantially biased
upward. A technique for dealing with this issue is discussed
in Chapter 18 (Performance Evaluation). Viewed as a two-
security portfolio with equal weighting, the return each
month is the average of the two individual returns. This
produces a portfolio return variance of 0.001118.

10. The value of the stocks is $117,380. Unless you know
precisely when the dividends are paid you cannot calculate an
exact answer. An approximate answer comes from the following
logic.

Period	Checks received	time invested	interest earned
1st qtr	$1174	≈ 10.5 months	$61.64
2nd qtr	$1174	≈ 7.5 months	44.03
3rd qtr	$1174	≈ 4.5 months	26.42
4th qtr	$1174	≈ 1.5 months	8.81
		total	$140.90

    Note that this figure is essentially half the amount that
would have been earned on 4% of the total portfolio value @
6% for one year. The lower figure reflects the fact that, on
average, the dividends are only invested half the year if the
dividend payment dates are uniformly spread over the calen-
dar.

11 - 13 Omitted

Chapter Fifteen

Revision of the Fixed Income Portfolio

KEY POINTS

Bond portfolios need revision just like stock portfolios. Note the Peter Bernstein quotation on the second page of the chapter.

There are two passive bond strategies: buy & hold and indexing. Buying and holding a bond portfolio, though, is not appropriate as securities mature and need to be replaced.

Classic active strategies include the laddered and barbell portfolios. The traditional advantage of these approaches is that the steps needed to adjust the portfolio are always known in advance.

Bond convexity is an advanced topic, although one that is receiving increasing interest among investment professionals. Convexity measures the extent to which duration changes as interest rates move.

TEACHING CONSIDERATIONS

While the laddered and barbell strategies are old hat, they are also classic: many institutions follow the practice of structuring their fixed income portfolios this way. This is a "basic principle" in the bond management business.

Depending on time constraints, you may want to spend some time on the notion of duration being a pure measure of interest rate risk only for parallel shifts in the yield curve. Convexity captures the error introduced from using duration alone. Students with a calculus background will be able to appreciate an analogy between speed and acceleration (the first and second derivatives of distance with respect to time) and duration and convexity (the first and second derivatives of the bond price with respect to interest rates). For students with prior familiarity with options, duration and convexity have analogies in delta and gamma.

Figure 15-8 shows the importance of increasing convexity in otherwise similar bonds. Bring up the idea of dominance with this figure.

ANSWERS TO QUESTIONS

1. Bonds mature and must be replaced. It is not prudent to hold actual cash. The funds must be reinvested.

2. Sometimes the absolute change in interest rates is different for long-term rates and short-term rates. A parallel shift involves every maturity changing by the same amount.

3. Stock can be bought and held; bonds cannot. For the long-term investor, the statement may be true.

4. Any default of a bond causes inconvenience and financial loss to the owner of the portfolio. The barbell and laddered portfolios are designed to deal with interest rate risk. The level of default risk the manager chooses to assume is a different matter entirely.

5. If short term rates are higher than any longer term rate, the curve is inverted.

6. Zero coupon bonds have no reinvestment rate risk. Therefore, their ultimate "behavior" is more predictable, and should be preferred in immunization strategies.

7. Yes. Otherwise identical securities should sell for a price that results in identical yields to maturity.

8. See question 1.

9. Risky bonds should always yield more than safer bonds. This means that the ratio of the yield on high grade bonds to the yield on low grade bonds should never be greater than one.

10. High. The higher the convexity, the more the portfolio benefits from a change in interest rates (as compared to a portfolio with a lower convexity).

11. There are higher order derivatives that are operative for very large changes in interest rates. Also, the shift in the yield curve may not be parallel, and nonparallel shifts reduce the accuracy of duration.

ANSWERS TO PROBLEMS

1. The interesting feature of the duration of an annuity is that the size of the cash flow is irrelevant. All that matters is the term of the cash flow stream and the discount rate. Refer to 4-12. In the denominator, P_0 is the present value of the cash flow stream, and this is the same as the formula for the present value of an annuity (equation 2-9). The duration of an annuity is therefore

$$D = \frac{1 + R}{R} - \frac{N}{(1+R)^N - 1}$$

Solving this problem as an ordinary annuity,

$$D = \frac{1.10}{.10} - \frac{20}{(1.10)^{20} - 1} = 11 - 3.49 = 7.51$$

Solving as an annuity due (which it probably would be),

$$D = \frac{1.10}{.10} - \frac{20}{(1.10)^{19} - 1} = 11 - 3.91 = 7.09$$

2. a. dollar weighted approach:

bond	value	duration	weighted duration
ABC	980	3.39	0.88
DEF	870	5.70	1.32
GHI	1020	8.79	2.38
JKL	900	9.11	2.17
Total	3770		6.75

b.   single security approach: yield to maturity = 6.87%
and duration = 11.34%

3. N = 4   C = 10%   P = 98   YTM = 10.03%

convexity = 21.97

4. modified duration = $\dfrac{D}{(1 + R/2)}$ = $\dfrac{3.39}{1 + .1063/2}$ = 3.22

a. using duration only: 3.22 x .005 = .0161 = 1.61%

b. using duration and convexity:

change from convexity = 21.97 x $(.005)^2$ = 0.000549
= 0.0549%

total change = 1.61% + .05% = 1.66% (to two decimals)

5. Omitted

6. Refer to Figure 15-5. The additional duration associated
with a lengthening maturity declines as maturity increases.
(This is what one of Malkiel's theorems states.) The barbell
portfolio is weighted more heavily in the early years, and so
these years receive a significant weight in the calculation
of portfolio duration. The barbell portfolio, therefore, has
less interest rate risk.

7. Duration = 9.50

8. The barbell portfolio might be composed of bonds with
very high coupons, or the size of the "weights" on the bar
might be very large. Either of these characteristics will
reduce the portfolio duration.

9. The point here is that you have control over the coupons
you select. You can choose lower coupons in the maturities
corresponding to the weights, and higher coupons on the bar.
There is no set size of the weights either, so you can tamper
with them to get the cash flow stream the way you want it.

10.   modified duration = $\dfrac{6.4}{1.055}$ = 6.07

$(-6.07 \times -0.005) + 125 \times (-.005)^2$ = 3.35%

Chapter Sixteen

Principles of Options and Option Pricing

KEY POINTS

The various uses of options in conservative portfolios are extremely important for the portfolio manager to understand. There is considerable misinformation about these assets, especially an impression that they are "risky" and imprudent.

Options are a good idea because they allow the risk and return characteristics of the portfolio to be shifted without wholesale changes in the portfolio itself. Options are created by individuals and institutional traders, not by the company represented by the underlying stock. Options give their owner the right, but not the obligation, to do something. This right can be exercised if it is advantageous to do so. If not, the option is allowed to expire, or is sold if time remains in its life.

Most of this chapter deals with basic principles. The meat of the options material comes in the following chapter and again later in the Portfolio Protection part of the book.

TEACHING CONSIDERATIONS

Stress the fact that options are not created by the underlying company. They are created by individual investors and by institutional traders. When someone buys a stock option on company XYZ for instance, XYZ receives no funds from the transaction.

It is also useful to point out that the economic justifi-cation for options (and most other derivative products) is risk transfer or the alteration of the risk/expected return characteristics of a particular investment. They are not merely "sidebets" on the future direction of the market.

If you have time in your course, the profit and loss diagrams are a useful way to reinforce the basic ideas under-lying these contracts.

Delta, the first derivative of the Black-Scholes option pricing model with respect to the stock price, is an extreme-ly important statistic. It will be exploited fully in the Portfolio Protection part of the book. Ensure that you spend a few minutes at this point showing that delta is a measure of how the price of an option changes as the value of the underlying asset changes.

The American Stock Exchange and the Chicago Board Options Exchange have several excellent videotapes available that can be productively employed in college courses. These are well-produced and objective; they are also inexpensive. You can get more information about these and other exchange products by calling their respective hotlines: for the AMEX, call 1-800-THE-AMEX; for the CBOE, call 1-800-OPTIONS.

ANSWERS TO QUESTIONS

1. A speculator who buys a call wants prices to advance. Some hedgers (such as a short seller) who buy a call do so as protection against rising prices.

2. False. The owner of an option has the right to do some-thing; the writer has an obligation to perform. Buying a call and writing a put are both bullish, but their risk and return characteristics are quite different.

3. Their value declines as time passes, everything else being equal.

4. False. One person can write multiple options; there does not have to be one writer for every buyer.

5. Exercise involves a commission expense and, for a call, the necessity to put up funds to buy stock. Most option users are interested in the profit potential or in the pro-tection characteristics they offer. It is not necessary to

exercise the options to enjoy these benefits.

6.   If someone writes an option (sells it as an opening transaction) and later buys an identical option, this eliminates the option position. This is because of the fungibility of the contracts.

7.   Buying a call has theoretically unlimited profit possibilities; writing a call, while also bullish, has a profit potential limited to the option premium. Buying a call has a known and limited maximum loss (the option premium); writing a put involves a potentially very large loss if the stock price declines precipitiously.

8.   Squibb JAN 115 call.

9.   Rising. Most of the striking prices are below the current stock price. As the stock price rises, the Options Clearing Corporation will add progressively larger striking prices to the list.

10.   Greater movement in the underlying stock price.

11.   Presumably, the right to exercise before expiration is valuable. If this is the case, American options should always sell for more than European options.

12.   All options have time value before expiration. Discrete pricing may make this unapparant in the financial pages.

13.   This is true by definition.

14.   This is false. The primary motivation for options is as a risk management tool. In particular, they allow for a security holder to alter the risk/expected return characteristics they face.

15.   Profits also can be made by selling the option before expiration day if the underlying stock price advances.

16.   False. An at-the-money option has intrinsic value equal to zero; it may, however, have a market value greater than zero that means it has time value.

17.   The out-of-the-money option may be long-term and have substantial time value whereas the in-the-money option is about to expire.

18.   Buying a put involves a known and limited maximum loss. Selling short involves a theoretically unlimited maximum loss.

19.   The normal definition of "writing" is selling an option as an opening transaction.   One would not normally use the term writing with the sale of a previously purchased option. Most market participants probably would say this statement is false.

20.   False.   As opening transactions are matched up, the open interest in a particular option declines.   New contracts can also be written, in which case option interest may go up.

21.   An in-the-money put gives the put owner something right out of the starting gate.   The stock price must rise sufficiently to move the put out-of-the-money.   The added riskiness of in-the-money put writing is reflected in the higher put premium.

22.   No.   Although this may seem logical, it does not work empirically nor is it born out by option pricing theory.

23.   1) time passed; 2) implied volatility has risen; 3) anticipated dividends have risen.

24.   Call premiums would rise.   Higher interest rates mean higher discount rates.   In the Black-Scholes options pricing model (Table 16-1) this increases the value of the call by reducing the present value of the striking price.   Interest rates matter because of arbitrage arguments such as those shown in the put/call parity example.

25.   The Options Clearing Corporation automatically adjusts the terms of options contracts such that there is no windfall gain or capricious loss to any option participant.   Holdings after the split are equivalent to those before the split.

26.   The boundary conditions involve a stock price of zero or a stock price of infinity.   At a stock price of zero, there is no incentive to buy the stock, and so the option premium will not move (delta = 0).   At an infinite stock price, the option premium also will be infinite.   When options have "substantial" intrinsic value, they act more and more like the underlying stock, and their delta approaches 1.0.

27.   Delta is equal to $N(d_1)$, which depends on interest rates.   So a change in interest rates will affect the delta,

although in practice this is a modest influence.

ANSWERS TO PROBLEMS

1.   a.   8 1/4 - 6 3/8 = 1 7/8

     b.   66 3/8 - 65 = 1 3/8

     c.   75 - 66 3/8 = 8 5/8

     d.   8 3/8, the option premium

     e.   115 - 85 3/8 - 4 1/4 = 25 3/8

     f.   unlimited

2.   If you buy the JNJ at the indicated price of 66 3/8:

400 x (57 3/8 - 66 3/8) + 200 (57 3/8 - 70) + 200 (5) = -5125
(loss on stock)   (loss on option)   (premium kept)

3. You have a gain:

400 x (77 3/8 - 66 3/8) + 200 (77 3/8 - 70) + 200 (5) = 6650

4.   There is nothing inherently wrong with this. This is a
bullish position with protection against losses and an added
gain if prices rise substantially. (This is the combination
of long stock and a put bull spread.)

5.   No gain on the stock; the puts expire worthless, meaning
that you lose the 2 5/8 paid for the 110 put but keep the 4
1/4 received from writing the 115 put. Your net gain is

          (4 1/4 - 2 5/8) x 100 = 162.50

6. $2.80

7.   15 APR 40 puts

8.   delta = -0.414

9.   Change the volatility estimate via trial and error until
the Black Scholes model predicts the put premium of $1 3/8.
The volatility used is then the implied volatility, and the
put delta can be read directly from the BSOPM file. As it
turns out, sigma is .26 and the put delta is -0.421.

Chapter Seventeen

Option Overwriting

KEY POINTS

Option overwriting is an increasingly popular portfolio activity by both individual and institutional investors. This is the option activity with which stockbrokers and other investment professionals are most familiar.

The writing of covered calls is an extremely important strategy that should be understood by everyone involved in the market. Writing puts is less common but is very appropriate for many investors.

Index options (rather than individual equity options) are preferred by many portfolio managers. Margin considerations make this activity potentially involved, but also potentially very rich.

Options can also be written to buy stock at a price lower than the currently prevailing price, or to sell stock at a higher than current price. In both cases the difference stems from time value of money implications.

TEACHING CONSIDERATIONS

Having discussed principles of options and options pricing, the main point of this chapter is to show how they are most commonly integrated into investment portfolios. Covered calls are widely used, are very useful, and, with index options, are potentially more sophisticated managerial tools than most people initially realize.

Go through an extended example showing how the margin rules provide different levels of income from call writing depending on the collateral used.

The notion of improving on the market should be discussed in detail. Be sure, however, to stress that this strategy does not in any way imply a market inefficiency. Capturing the time value involves a time value of money tradeoff.

ANSWERS TO QUESTIONS

1. Declining prices make put overwriting dangerous. Precipitous declines can be disastrous to put writers, as some people discovered during the crash of 1987.

2. The tradeoff is simple: the lower the striking price of a call, the higher its premium, but the greater the likelihood of it being exercised. An option writer would earn more premium by writing the APR 70, but would also have a higher risk of exercise.

3. An in-the-money put stands a greater chance of exercise than an out-of-the-money put. The stock price must advance further with an in-the-money put before it ceases to have intrinsic value.

4. Covered calls can be used in any portfolio which contains common stock. Writing covered calls is attractive during periods of declining market prices or when market prices are flat.

5. The portfolio manager need not worry about individual equity positions being called away if index options are written. Also, the manager does not need to keep track of many different positions; it is much easier to follow a single index such as the S&P 100.

6. This would be very reasonable and is often done. Both writing calls and buying puts are bearish strategies, and there is no reason they cannot be done simultaneously.

7. With covered calls, the maximum loss is known and limited. With naked calls, however, potential losses are theoretically unlimited. An unlimited loss would put the charitable organization out of business.

8. Omitted.

9. As stated in the text, the term "short put" is somewhat ambiguous. For margin purposes, a put is covered if the put writer has on deposit cash or cash equivalents whose market value equals 100% of the strike price.

10. This makes sense to me. If the short put is exercised, the put writer must buy shares, conceivably at a loss. But the short stock position would hedge this loss entirely. The shares purchased could immediately be delivered against the short position.

11. With a fiduciary put, the exercise price is escrowed. In the event of exercise, the put writer already has the funds to buy the stock. Non-fiduciary puts do not offer this protection.

12. You cannot say that writing index puts is always prefer-able to writing individual equity calls. Sometimes company-specific events make it appropriate to write individual equity calls, sometimes a portfolio is too small to permit the writing of even a single covered index call, and some-times regulatory policy precludes the use of index options.

13. Omitted.

14. If the plan is to buy stock, the option writer wants a high likelihood that the options will be exercised. The more the option is in-the-money, the greater the likelihood of exercise. So presumably the in-the-money put is preferred.

15. At expiration someone holds the valuable put. Whoever holds it when the music stops is going to exercise it. Otherwise they would be throwing money away.

ANSWERS TO PROBLEMS

1. See attached.

2. Gain on stock: 400 x (77 3/8 - purchase price)

    Options expire worthless: gain = 2 x 2 1/2 x 100 = 500

3. See attached.

4. See attached.

Problem 17-1

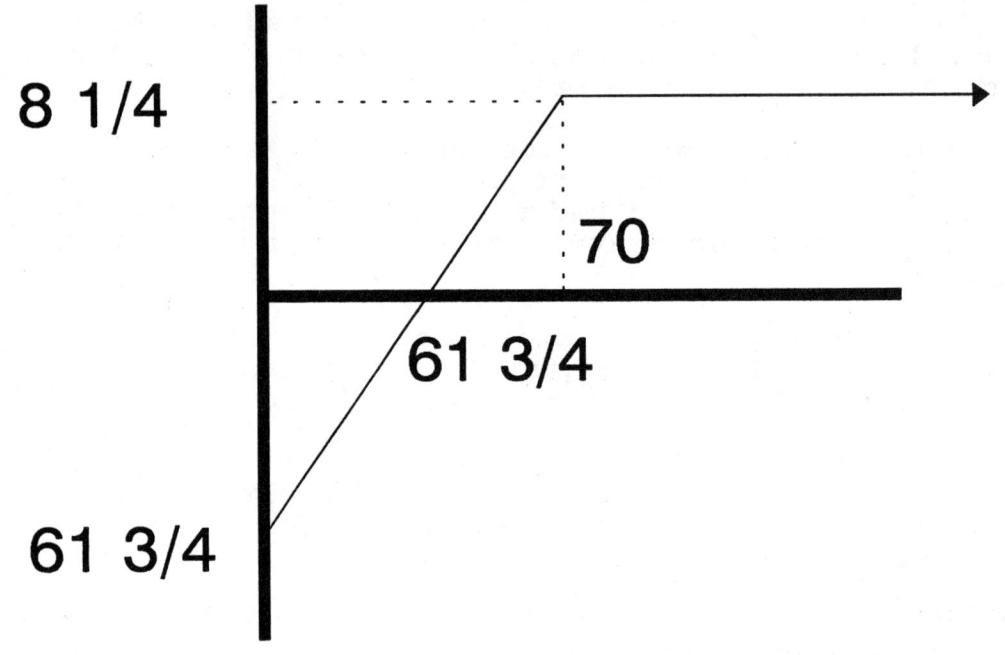

8 1/4

70

61 3/4

61 3/4

Problem 17-3

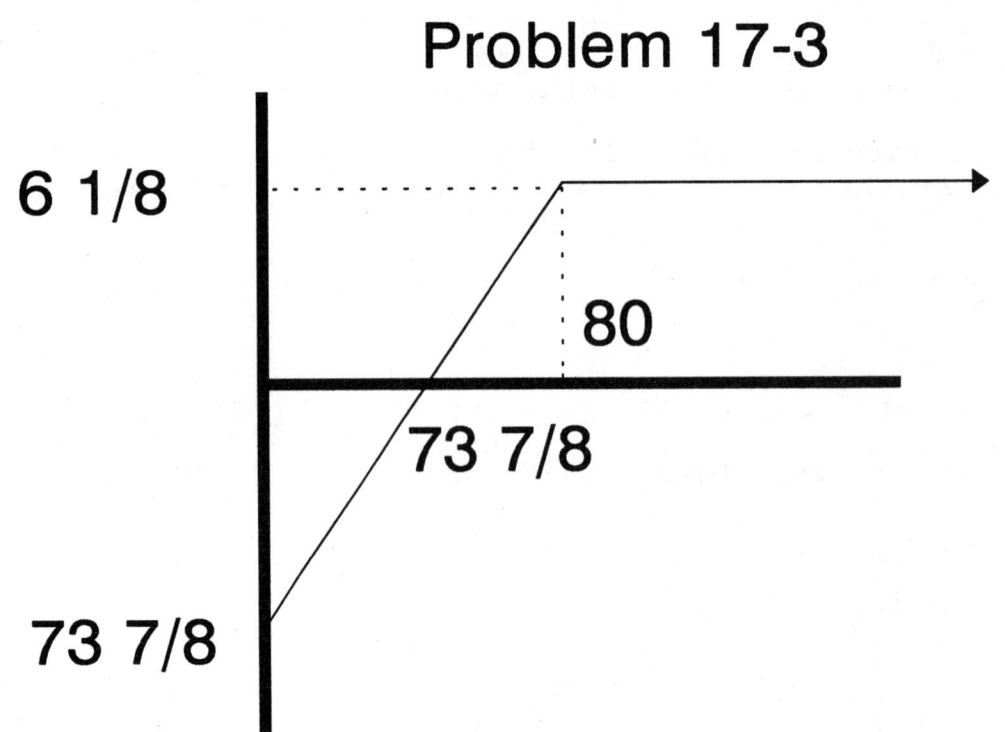

6 1/8

80

73 7/8

73 7/8

Problem 17-4

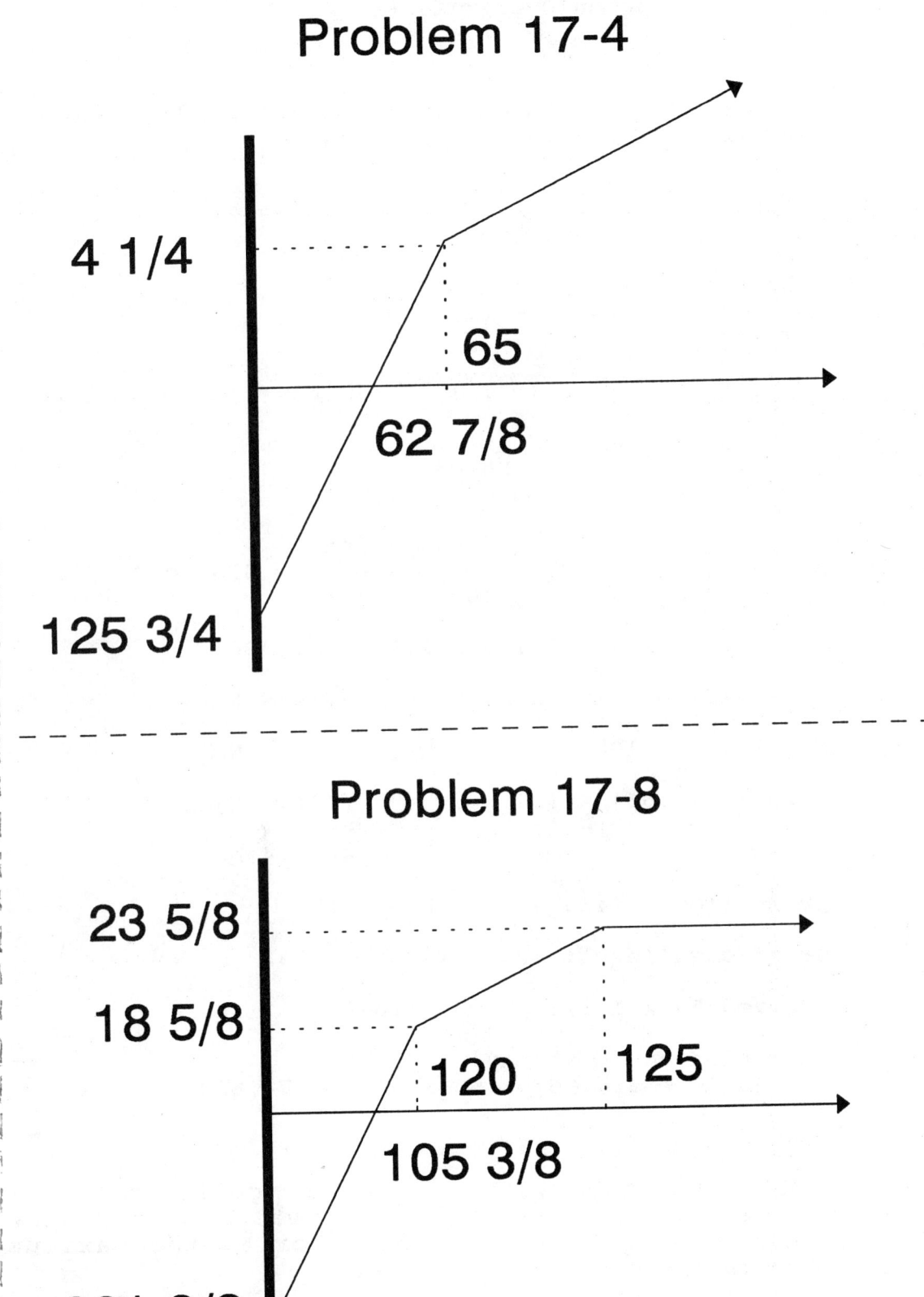

4 1/4

65

62 7/8

125 3/4

Problem 17-8

23 5/8

18 5/8

120

125

105 3/8

221 3/8

5. a. You paid $27,000; income received was $3,000, and the
capital gain was also $3,000. Therefore,

$$HPR = \frac{30,000 - 27,000 + 3000}{27,000} = 22.2\%$$

b. $$\frac{3000}{(1+R)^{60}} + \frac{30000}{(1+R)^{78}} - 27000 = 0$$

        This gives a daily R of 0.00263. To annualize,
multiply by 365:

$$.00263 \times 365 = 96.0\%$$

6. a. Maximum # of calls: $$\frac{10 \text{ million}}{100 \times 315.66} = 316 \text{ contracts}$$

        316 contracts x $ 1 1/8 x 100 = $35,500

    b. .15 x 315.66 x 100 x N   =   4734.9 N
                    plus
        N x 1 1/8 x 100   =   112.5 N
                    minus
        (320 - 315.66) x 100 x N   =   (434.0 N)
                                          _____
                                           4413.4 N

        10 million = 4413.4 N   N = 2265

    c. 50% of cash level: 2265 x .50 = 1132

7. You received 50 x 1 1/8 x 100 = 5625

    At expiration you must pay
            (320.00 - 334.96) x 50 x 100 = $74,800

8. See attached.

9. Presumably the stock will be used for collateral in a
margin account. Stock counts half the value of cash for
margin purposes. You can then solve for N, the maximum
number of contracts that can be written:

$$N\left[[298.96 \times 15\% \times 100]+[(300-298.96) \times 100]+[7 \ 3/4 \times 100]\right] =$$

.5 x $5 million

$$N = 466 \text{ contracts}$$

$$466 \text{ contracts} \times 7 \ 3/4 \times 100 = \$361,150$$

10.   The market rose $\dfrac{308 - 298.96}{298.96}$ = 3.02%.

The   portfolio should rise by
1.15 x 3.02% = 3.48%, or $69,600.

Gain on the 310 calls:
2 x 100 x ($3 - 0) =   600

Gain on the 305 puts:
2 x 100 x (9 3/8 - 0) =   1,875
                                             ─────────
                           total $72,075

11.   Assume the 315 put sells for its intrinsic value of
16.04.   (Alternatively, you could compute an implied volatility using the AUG 315 calls and use this to estimate a premium.)

$$N\left[[298.96 \times 15\% \times 100]+[(315-298.96) \times 100]+[16.04 \times 100]\right] =$$

.5 x $5 million

$$N = 324 \text{ contracts}$$

$$324 \text{ contracts} \times 16.04 \times 100 = \$519,696$$

12.

$$N\left[[298.96 \times 15\% \times 100]+[(300-298.96) \times 100]+[10 \times 100]\right] =$$

.5 x $5 million

$$N = 464 \text{ contracts}$$
$$464 \text{ contracts} \times 10 \times 100 = \$464,000$$

Chapter Eighteen

Performance Evaluation

KEY POINTS

Performance evaluation is a critical part of the portfolio management process, but one that is often casually done or overlooked altogether.

Any measurement of performance should somehow tie together the return of the investment and the riskiness of that return. The popular press very often focuses only on return, largely ignoring risk.

The Sharpe and Treynor performance measures are classic elements of performance evaluation, and are useful. They become less useful when there are additions to or withdrawals from the portfolio. In such a case the internal rate of return becomes the appropriate measure of return.

The presence of options in a portfolio complicates the performance evaluation process. Two methods for comparing an optioned portfolio with an unoptioned counterpart are the Residual Option Spread and the Incremental Rate of Return from Options.

TEACHING CONSIDERATIONS

There are two key points that must be clear to students after this discussion. First, the performance of a portfolio cannot be determined in the absence of information about the riskiness of the portfolio. The popular financial press

routinely reports which mutual funds "did best" by ranking
them by their realized returns from the previous year. Such
a procedure ignores very real differences in volatility (and
consequently investor utility) associated with them.

The other key point is the return that counts is that
which is realized from an increase in the market value of the
portfolio and from income received. A portfolio that receives a cash inflow will show an increase in value, but not
one attributable to the fund management. Similarly, if funds
are withdrawn from the portfolio, this should not count
against the manager's performance evaluation.

I recommend the 44 Wall Street & Mutual Shares comparison
discussed in the chapter. This is an effective case study
showing the additional information provided by volatility
information.

ANSWERS TO QUESTIONS

1.   Risk, by definition, is the chance of loss. A risky
situation involves an uncertain outcome, and some possible
outcomes are adverse. Repeated draws from the probability
distribution will periodically result in the selection of an
adverse outcome. It is important to know something about the
distribution before choosing to draw one. Because you were
lucky once does not mean you will be again.

2.   Investors like return and dislike risk. Utility comes
from getting more return and reducing risk. Securities are
priced to provide a level of return consistent with their
perceived level of risk. Over the long term, a portfolio of
risky securities should earn a higher return than a safer
portfolio. Some portfolio components, however, probably will
be losers. Risk-adjusted performance measurement seeks to
associate a measure of the likelihood of loss with the return
statistic.

3.   Investors do not like risk. Everything else being equal,
they prefer the least risky alternative.

4.   You would want to know how long it took to double, and
what its interim price behavior looked like. It also would
be useful to compare the security to the return and risk of a
market index over the same period.

5.   Examples include legal lists of eligible investments,
regulatory constraints, special tax incentives/disincentives,

and statutory restrictions (the state of Indiana, for instance, once disallowed any common stock investments in its
retirement fund).

6.   It makes no difference.   The geometric mean return is
invariant to the order of the returns.

7.   a.   arithmetic
     b.   geometric
     c   geometric or arithmetic, depending on what you were
          going to do with the information

8.   Returns can be negative.   You cannot take an even root of
a negative number, and if you have an odd number of negative
returns the geometric mean will be an imaginary number.
Return relatives are only positive.

9.   When looking at a single security, it is best to use the
Treynor measure, as the market only rewards you for bearing
systematic risk.   The Treynor measure is based on beta, which
measures systematic risk.

10.   Do the calculations monthly or quarterly, and ignore
time value of money considerations in the interim.   Little
accuracy is lost in doing so.

11.   Writing covered calls partially offsets changes in the
value of the portfolio either up or down.   This attenuates
the volatility of the portfolio.

ANSWERS TO PROBLEMS

1. $\bar{x}_a = .026$ $\sigma_a = .0459$ $SH_a = \dfrac{.026 - .03}{.0459} = -.087$

   $\bar{x}_b = .032$ $\sigma_b = .0462$ $SH_b = \dfrac{.032 - .03}{.0462} = .0433$

   $\bar{x}_c = .040$ $\sigma_c = .0927$ $SH_c = \dfrac{.040 - .03}{.0927} = .1079$

2.   The annual returns of the equally-weighted portfolio are
5%, 0%, -.33%, 12%, and 5,67%.   Their mean is 4.47% with
a standard deviation of .0450.   The Sharpe measure is then

$$SH_p = \frac{.0447 - .03}{.0450} = .3267$$

See the attached graph.

3. A: $(1.05)(1.0)(.95)(1.08)(1.05)^{.2} - 1 = .0250$

B: $(1.04)(1.01)(.96)(1.10)(1.05)^{.2} - 1 = .0310$

C: $(1.06)(.99)(.90)(1.18)(1.07)^{.2} - 1 = .0358$

Port.: $(1.05)(1.0)(.9967)(1.12)(1.0567)^{.2} - 1 = .0437$

Ranking by geometric mean:

Portfolio (best)
C
B
A (worst)

4. Using Lotus 1-2-3, the monthly IRR is 0.0026, for an annual rate of 3.12%.

5. See attached graph.

6. IRAR = $(SH_o - SH_u)\sigma_o = (.0433 - (-.087))(.0462) = 0.0060$

7. $-783000 + \sum\limits_{t=1}^{12} \frac{4550}{(1+R)^t} + \frac{773000}{(1+R)^{12}} = 0$

R = 0.004776 per month, or 5.73% per year.

8. Omitted.

Problem 18-2

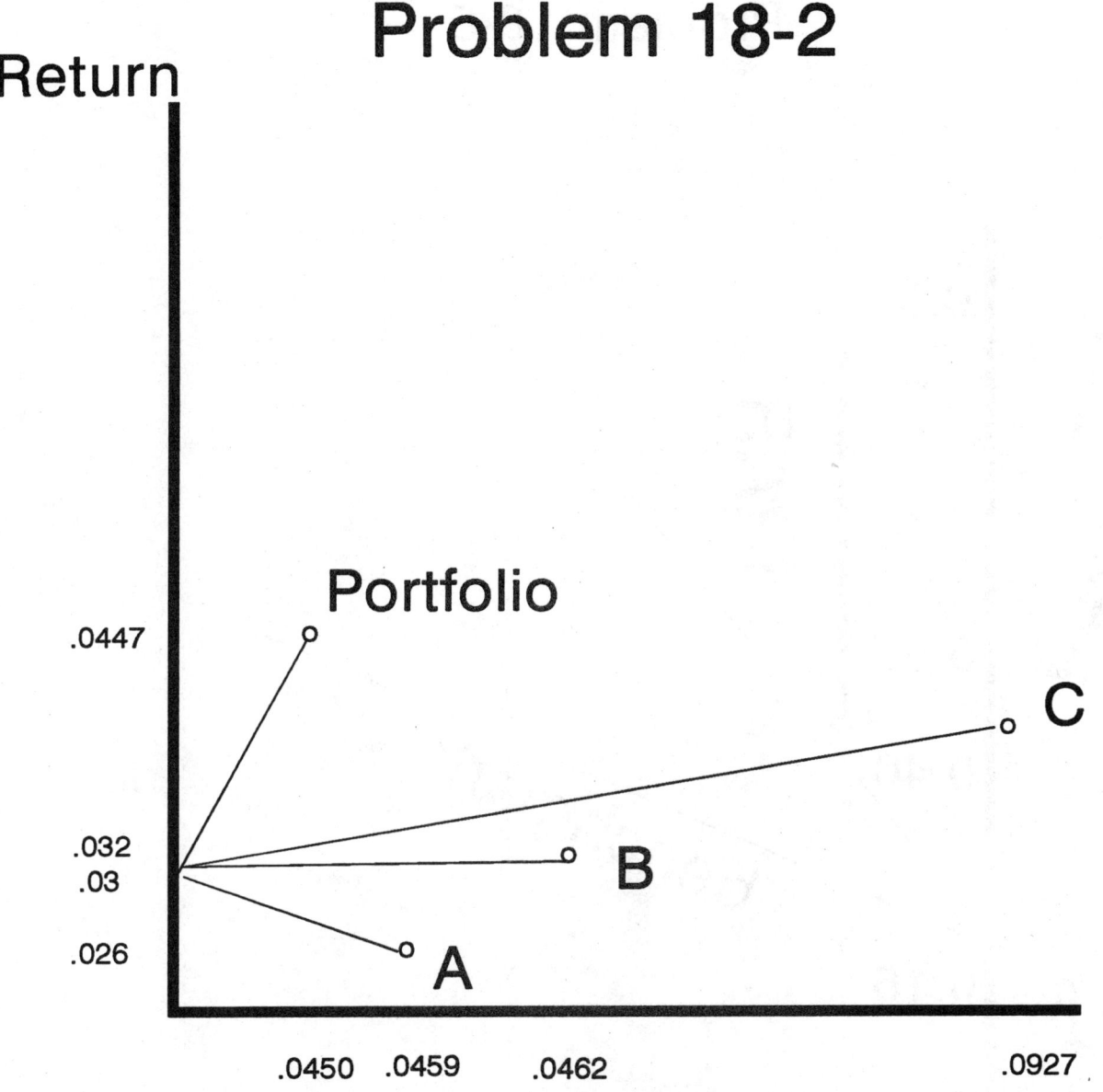

Problem 18-5

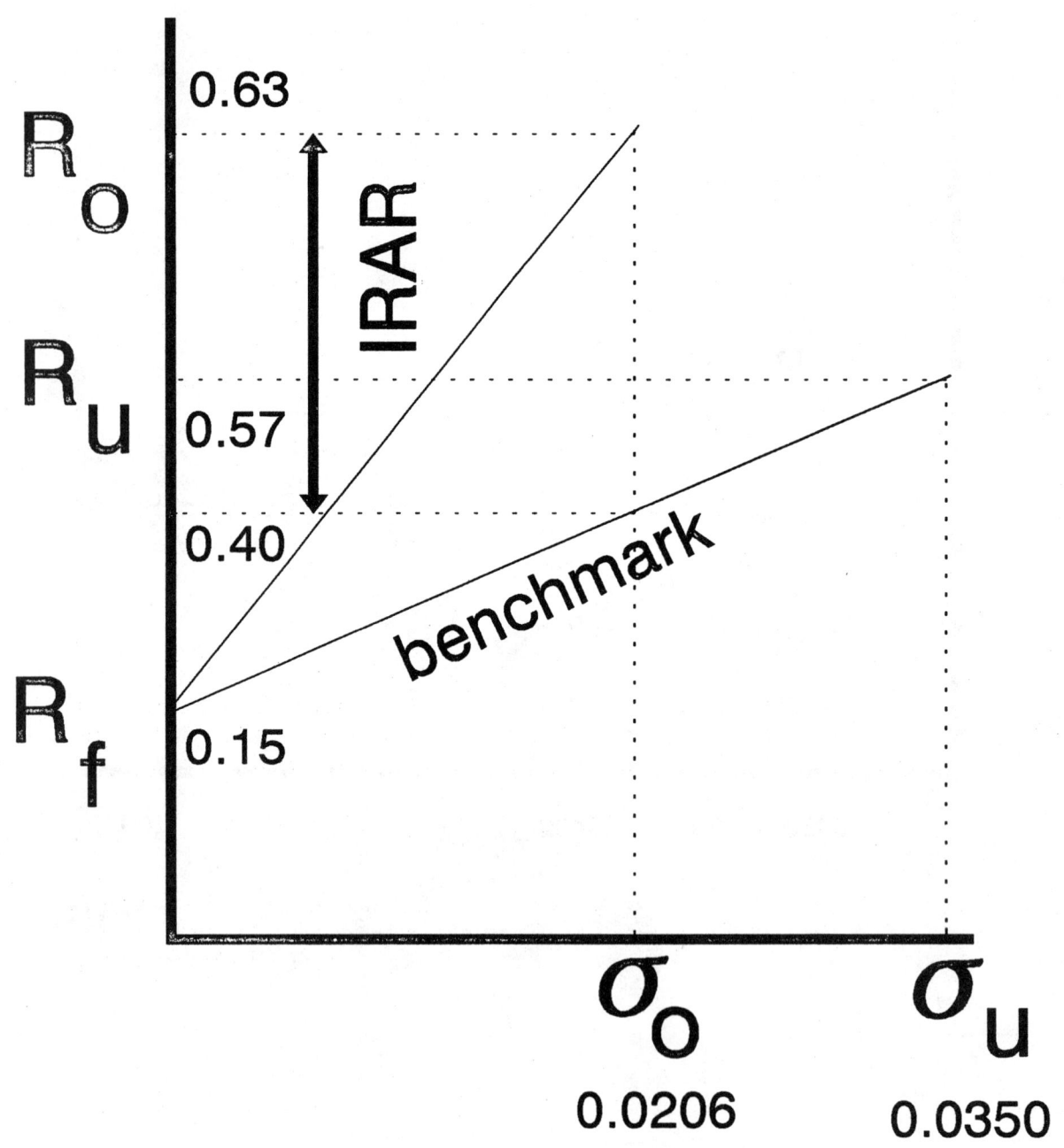

Chapter Nineteen

Principles of the Futures Market

KEY POINTS

The futures market is a very misunderstood part of our economic system. Its primary purpose is enabling hedgers to reduce risk they find unacceptable and transfer it to someone else (usually a speculator) who is willing to bear it. Speculators do so because they believe they will earn a profit by taking the risk.

Unlike options, futures contracts are promises. The buyer promises to pay, while the seller promises to deliver a quantity of the commodity. While a delivery process is essential to a well-functioning futures market, most futures contracts are eliminated by an offsetting transaction before the delivery month.

TEACHING CONSIDERATIONS

Ensure that students understand why we have futures markets. You may want to use an insurance analogy to illustrate risk transfer. People reduce or eliminate risks by buying insurance, thereby transferring the risk to the insurance company.

The exchanges have excellent videotapes useful in reinforcing basic principles of the futures market. Several of my favorites are "The Financial Marketplace," 17 minutes, Chicago Mercantile Exchange; "The Trading Floor," Chicago Board of Trade; and "Fundamentals of Futures (5 in 1), 45 minutes, Chicago Board of Trade.

ANSWERS TO QUESTIONS

1. The same contract can be traded often. A single contract
represents an open interest of one, but if it is traded five
times in one day this is volume of five contracts.

2. It is the delivery option that causes the futures price
and the cash price to converge in the delivery month. The
pricing of futures would be less certain if delivery were not
an option.

3. There is disagreement about this. On the one hand they
seem to preclude the market finding a new equilibrium price
as quickly as it would like. On the other hand, they probably reduce panic trading when prices move sharply and provide
a time-out so that trades can be made based on accurate news
rather than rumors.

4. Hedgers are users or producers of a product; their activities are usually considered less risky than those of the
speculator. To the extent this is the case, the lower mar-
gins make sense.

5. If the basis narrows, this means the futures price and
the cash price have moved closer together. This can happen
for several reasons, such as the passage of time or a decline
in interest rates or carrying costs. Many hedgers choose to
remove their hedge before the delivery month and deliver the
commodity locally. A decline in interest rates or carrying
costs often is of general benefit to the hedger.

6. As in question 1, a given contract can trade more than
once. There is no necessary relationship between open interest and trading volume.

7. The futures exchanges enable the farmer (and other users)
to reduce price risk. If they had to carry the full risk of
a bad crop year, they would have to charge a higher price for
their commodity to compensate for the off-years.

8. Is there a hedgeable interest? How many potential users
of the product are there? Would the contract attract speculators? (If it would not attract speculators, it is not
likely to succeed.)

9. There is debate about this, but the open outcry system seems very well suited to the trading of futures contracts. Computerized trading (such as that at the New Zealand Futures Exchange and that associated with the new GLOBEX system) is more likely to replace the marketmaker system than is the specialist system.

10. Lettuce is non-fungible. Even in the grocery store, adjacent heads of lettuce are not equally desirable to the consumer. It would be difficult to describe adequately the characteristics of lettuce deliverable against such a contract.

11. There are 5,000 bushels in one contract: a) selling 8 contracts would be less than a 100% hedge, and this is what most hedgers would do; b) selling 10 contracts would be a 100% hedge, which is also okay; c) selling 12 contracts would be over-hedging, which is essentially speculating on the two odd contracts.

12. a. a cereal manufacturer
     b. a manufacturer of class rings
     c. a soybean processor who produces soy oil and soy
         meal

13. This is because of the cost of carry. If more distant delivery months did not cost more than the near months, it would not be economic to store goods for future consumption. This would lead to oversupply short term, which would depress the spot price. Near-term delivery prices would then again be below far-term delivery month prices.

14. If someone anticipated receiving foreign currency at a specific point in the future, the foreign exchange risk could be reduced by a short hedge in which the hedger promised to deliver the foreign currency at a predetermined price.

15. Refer to Table 19-3. If the local currency rate (the German rate) rises, the futures price will decline. So this is not good news to the DM speculator.

ANSWERS TO PROBLEMS

1. $\dfrac{(\$6.32 - \$6.30)}{\text{bushel}} \times 4 \text{ contracts} \times \dfrac{5000 \text{ bu.}}{\text{contract}} = \$400$

2.   a.   No money is received by the hedger at the time the hedge is established when using the futures market.

b. $$\frac{\$6.32}{bu} \times 8 \text{ contracts} \times \frac{5000 \text{ bu}}{contract} = \$252,800$$

3.   The futures price is the best estimate of the future cash price according to the expectations hypothesis.

4. $$DM \text{ } 8 \text{ million} \times \frac{contract}{DM \text{ } 125,000} = 64 \text{ contracts}$$

5.   If interest rates rise by 0.5% in Leptonia relative to the US (perhaps because of inflation fears), Leptons will likely depreciate by 0.5% relative to the US dollar. If the initial rate is $0.4817/Lepton, the new rate will be

$$\$0.4817 \times 1.005 = \$0.4841$$

6.   The spot rate is missing here; assume it is $0.5701/DM, the same as the September futures that cease trading in a few weeks. Foreign exchange futures cease trading on the 2nd business day immediately preceding the 3rd Wednesday of the contract month. In 1991, this meant the December futures ceased trading 111 days after the newspaper date. Use the formula in Table 19-3:

$$.5652 = .5701 \times [1 + (.0606 - I_{lc}) \times 111/365)]$$

$$I_{lc} = 8.88\%$$

7. $$\frac{(\$0.5610 - .5600)}{DM} \times 3 \text{ contracts} \times \frac{DM \text{ } 125000}{contract} = \$375 \text{ gain}$$

8.   If the DM are delivered against the futures contracts there are no cash market transactions. The hedger went short at $0.5622; this is the realized price when the DM are delivered. Had the hedge not been used, the realized price would have been $0.5610. Hedging resulted in a gain of

$$\frac{(\$0.5622 - .5610)}{DM} \times 8 \text{ contracts} \times \frac{DM\ 125000}{\text{contract}} = \$1,200 \text{ gain}$$

Chapter Twenty

Benching the Equity Players

KEY POINTS

It is possible to remove market risk from the portfolio without selling the components. This can be done using equity options, index options, or the futures market.

Risk is removed by hedging. Hedging involves establishing a second position whose price behavior will likely offset the price behavior of the original portfolio.

Delta enables the portfolio manager to figure out the number of option contracts necessary to mimic the returns of the underlying security. This statistic is important in the calculation of many hedge ratios.

Dynamic hedging involves monitoring a portfolio's position delta and readjusting this value as it deviates from a target number.

TEACHING CONSIDERATIONS

The idea of delta is crucial in portfolio protection, and it is essential that this point gets across to the student. Explain that a delta of 0.60, for instance, means that the option will rise by 60 cents for every $1 rise in the value of the underlying asset.

The insurance policy example used with the protective put is effective; students seem to remember this analogy.   Con-

trast a protective put with a covered call, stressing how
they provide very different levels of protection.

Stress also that index options are much simpler to employ
in the removal of market risk than individual equity options.
The OEX contract is the tool of choice for many professional
portfolio risk managers.

Emphasize that the S&P500 futures contract is similar to
traditional agricultural futures, except that delivery does
not occur, nor does it need to occur for this to be an effective hedging tool. When discussing the hedge ratio, reinforce the notion that the main idea is to build a second
portfolio which will offset, fully or in part, the gains or
losses in the primary investment portfolio.

Finally, spend some time on the position delta idea as
shown in the Portfolio Memo. Familiarity with position delta
is the first step in understanding the emerging area of
financial engineering.

ANSWERS TO QUESTIONS

1. The objective is the temporary removal of some or all the
market risk associated with a portfolio. Portfolio protection techniques are generally more economic in terms of
commissions and managerial time than the sale and eventual
replacement of portfolio components.

2. You can "fine-tune" the likely price behavior of a portfolio by altering its market risk (as measured by the position delta). Writing options will, in addition, alter the
income stream the portfolio produces.

3. Delta indicates the quantity of a particular option
necessary to replicate the underlying asset.   There is some
quantity of call options, for instance, which (for modest
movements in the underlying asset price) behaves like the
underlying asset itself.

4. Buying a protective put to protect the value of a long
stock position.

5. The value of the stock index is merely a marker repre-
senting the current value of the underlying basket of stocks.
While delivery conceivably could occur with a stock index, it
is not necessary. Because of the guaranty provision of the
option contract provided by the Options Clearing Corporation,

index option users can settle their positions in cash.

6.   Protective puts provide protection against large price declines, whereas covered calls provide only limited downside protection.   Covered calls bring in the option premium, while the protective put requires a cash outlay.

7.   An S&P500 stock index futures contract has a delta of 1.0 because the S&P _is_ the market, practically speaking.   Short futures contracts add negative deltas to a portfolio.

8.   Yes.   There is likely to be substantial unsystematic risk in the five-security portfolio, however, which the futures contract could not hedge.

9.   The higher the portfolio beta the greater the anticipated price volatility of the portfolio, and so the greater the number of options or futures that are needed to hedge the portfolio.

10.   As time passes, the value of a stock index futures contract will decline even if the underlying stock index does not change.   This is because of the time value of money.   The short hedger benefits from a price decline, so the declining basis works to their benefit.

11.   A put has a negative delta; so does a short position in stock.   The right quantity of shares sold short will behave the same as a particular put.   A put contract with a delta of -0.450, for instance, behaves the same as 45 shares sold short.

12.   Dynamic hedging is a process in which the position delta of a portfolio is routinely adjusted to return it to some target level.   The passage of time and the changing value of the underlying asset are two primary reasons why the portfolio needs periodic revision to stay on track.

13.   Insurance connotes a contractual arrangement.   In the market crash of 1987 the market did not behave as arbitrage arguments suggest it was "supposed" to.   Insurance provides protection with little risk of insurance company default. Investment portfolios based on delta and the behavior of market prices are more risky than a contractual insurance contract.   Some people who thought their portfolios were insured found that they were not.

14.   No; this is commonly done.

15. Hedging involves reducing or eliminating risk. Once the risk is removed, any further hedging amounts to speculation.

ANSWERS TO PROBLEMS

1. (10000 x 1.0) + (50 x 100 x -0.181) = 9095

2. 10000 + (N x 100 x -.181) = 0   N = 552 contracts

            552 contracts x $0.50 x 100 = $27,600

3. 10000 - (100 x .819 x 100) = 1810

4. The problem omitted the striking price; use 325.

$$HR = \frac{\text{Portfolio value}}{\text{Contract value}} \times \beta \times \frac{1}{|\text{delta}|}$$

$$= \frac{\$2.5 \text{ million}}{325 \times \$100} \times 1.12 \times \frac{1}{.223} = 386.34$$

5. New hedge ratio:

$$= \frac{\$2.45 \text{ million}}{325 \times \$100} \times 1.12 \times \frac{1}{.245} = 344.61$$

      Sell 42 puts

6. $$\frac{\$2.5 \text{ million}}{357.60 \times \$500} \times 1.12 = 15.66$$

      Sell 15 or 16 contracts

7 - 9. Omitted

10.   a. The value declines to converge on the intrinsic
           value.
       b. The value declines to converge on zero.
       c. The value declines to converge on the intrinsic
           value.
       d. The value declines to converge on zero.

11. $delta_{call} = 1 - |delta_{put}|$

   Stated another way, the absolute values of the put and call deltas sum to 1.0.

Chapter Twenty-One

Removing Interest Rate Risk

KEY POINTS

This chapter is a cousin to the previous one. Just as market risk can be removed from the equity portfolio, interest rate risk can be removed or reduced from the fixed income portfolio.

Interest rate risk is most commonly reduced either by creating a hedge with interest rate futures contracts or by portfolio dedication. When futures are used, it is necessary to calculate a hedge ratio in the same fashion as with stock index futures; the duration statistic is needed rather than beta.

Treasury bond futures are priced (and hedges should be constructed) based on the price of the cheapest to deliver bond. Correction factors are used to compensate for the fact that bonds have different coupons, maturities, and durations, and therefore are not all equally desirable.

Portfolios can be immunized against interest rate risk by altering their duration. The two broad classes of immunization are bullet immunization and the bank immunization case.

TEACHING CONSIDERATIONS

Many students will find risk reduction in the fixed income portfolio to be less intellectually comfortable than risk reduction in the equity portfolio. Refresh memories of duration, interest rate risk, and the relationship between them.

The material on the characteristics of the interest rate futures is provided as background to increase the likelihood that students will not approach the business of immunization in "black box" fashion. Ensure that people understand what the T bond contract involves.

The cheapest to deliver discussion is a good example of the market's awareness of the potential for arbitrage and its willingness to exploit arbitrage opportunities quickly. Table 21-3 can be helpful in clarifying the idea. Explain logically how two deliverable bonds may have different appeal, and how the Chicago Board of Trade correction factors deal with this possibility.

The information in Table 21-4 is very helpful in illustrating the idea of reinvestment rate risk and how a duration matched portfolio eliminates interest rate risk and reinvestment rate risk.

Although it is not a strict portfolio management topic, I like to cover the bank immunization case example briefly, as many students are likely to consider a banking career.

ANSWERS TO QUESTIONS

1. Everything else being equal, investors prefer higher coupons to lower, and higher yield to maturities to lower one. Correction factors, in theory, make all bonds equally attractive by making some bonds "count more" in the delivery process with T bond futures.

2. The bond equivalent yield adjusts for the fact that there are 365 days (not 360) in a year and the T-bill investment requires initial payment of the discounted price, not the par value.

3. The yield curve does not always experience a parallel shift. There is likely to be tracking error if a short-term portfolio is hedged using a long-term instrument.

4. A callable bond is not equivalent to a non-callable bond. If there is a preference for one investment over another, the two will not sell for the same price. The T-bond futures contract is based on bonds that are non-callable in the near term.

5.   The manager of a money market portfolio, the corporate treasurer who was holding an unusually large cash balance, or the investment officer who anticipated a purchase of money market securities in the near future and wanted to lock in the current rate.

6.   Interest rates might move in your favor, in which case you will have an opportunity loss. Also, a lower duration usually results in a lower portfolio yield, and transactions costs probably will be incurred.

7.   The need to hedge long-term rates is probably more important, although this depends on your perspective.

8.   The hedge would be less than ideal for the same reasons mentioned in problem 3.

9.   Using the logic of Table 21-3, the fewer bonds you would have to deliver (for a given bond price), the better to you.

10.   This is false. The productof interest sensitive asset dolla

11.   Settlement prices differ for the various delivery months because of anticipation of changing interest rates and because of the structure of the yield curve.

ANSWERS TO PROBLEMS

1.   93.33 ==> 93.33% of par == .9333 x $1 million = $933,330

2.   A change of one basis point = $25.

$$\frac{6 \text{ basis points}}{\text{contract}} \text{ x 4 contracts x } \frac{\$25}{\text{bp}} = \$600$$

3.   Duration equals the maturity.

4.   Omitted.

5.   a.   From equation 21-2,

   $10000 = $9800 - discount amount

   discount amount = $200

$$\text{discount amount} = \text{face value} \times \frac{\text{days}}{360} \times \text{ask discount}$$

$$\$200 = \$10000 \times \frac{88}{360} \times \text{ask discount}$$

$$\text{ask discount} = .0818 = 8.18\%$$

Chapter Twenty-Two

Integrating Derivative Assets and Portfolio Management

KEY POINTS

This chapter functions as an extended case study reviewing how a portfolio manager might productively employ derivative assets to alter the risk of a portfolio or to enhance its yield.

The example deals with a portfolio containing both equity securities and fixed income securities, and shows how a linear program can be used for construction of the constrained stock portfolio.

Index calls can increase the yield of a portfolio, and they are used for that purpose here. Both market and company specific risk are reduced. It is possible to minimize the cash outlay in a risk management application by proper selection of the puts and calls (and possibly futures) used. Simultaneous equations can be solved to get a desired position delta at minimum cost.

Options also can be used with the fixed income portfolio, and the chapter briefly discusses the use of T-bond options.

TEACHING CONSIDERATIONS

This chapter can accomplish quite a bit, and I suggest you avoid having to cram it in during the last week of class. Ensure that you reserve enough time to go over this example carefully. It provides a good review of much of the techni-

cal risk management material provided in earlier chapters, and
reinforces how options can be used to augment portfolio
income.

If your students can do so, a homework problem using SAS
to solve a portfolio linear program is a useful exercise.
(PORTMAN also will solve such a problem, but you may consider
it useful to reinforce the process by using the linear program.)

I like the example problem in Table 22-11. The use of
simultaneous equations to achieve your desired position delta
and do so with little cash outlay is a worthy exercise.

ANSWERS TO QUESTIONS

1. Writing index calls does not influence the value of the
stock portfolio itself in any way. However, writing calls
can result in a financial liability if they close in-the-
money. Calls become in-the-money when the stock market
rises, so presumably the stock portfolio rose as well if the
index calls became valuable. It is likely that the "loss" on
the calls is largely offset by a gain on the stock, so in
practice the price appreciation of the total portfolio is
limited.

2. The lower the striking price the higher the premium
income, but the greater the likelihood of exercise. Logically, high striking prices yield little income, but are seldom
exercised. High striking prices also have low deltas, which
means they provide only a modest adjustment to position
delta. In-the-money options, which have high deltas, are
powerful tools in altering the portfolio risk.

3. Index or equity puts could have been written.

4. Individual equity options are useful in hedging company-
specific risk. They are also useful for generating income in
small portfolios that are not sufficiently valuable to provide the necessary collateral for option writing.

5. There is disagreement over which is riskier, writing
individual calls or index calls. A good argument can be made
that writing individual equity calls is riskier, as a single
security sometimes has a spectacular one-day gain, rising by
perhaps 50% because of takeover news. The stock market has
never experienced a gain of this size. Option writers are

hurt by rapidly rising prices, and because equity options can rise faster than index options, a good argument can be made that the margin requirements should be stiffer on individual options. (If the equity option is covered, of course, the risk of a rapid price rise is eliminated.)

6. First, figure out the market value and beta of the portfolio to be hedged. Then select a striking price for the put depending on the level of protection desired. Next, calculate the delta of the desired option. (This may require calculating implied volatility first.) Finally, calculate the hedge ratio as shown on page 443.

7. At-the-money futures puts and calls sell for the same price.

8. Writing calls is a bearish strategy when done in isolation. From the writer's perspective, gains accrue when the value of the underlying asset declines. Combining this strategy with a long position in the underlying asset reduces the market exposure in the underlying asset, because the short option will offset some gains that might be experienced without the options.

9. Option prices are not a linear function of the underlying stock price. The 0.5% decline results in the option falling in value by $0.93, while a 0.5% rise results in an option price rise of only $0.50. This difference is primarily because the option was not initially at-the-money.

ANSWERS TO PROBLEMS

1 - 3 Omitted.

4. The portfolio in the chapter initially had an income shortfall of $16,624. The AUG 315 calls have a premium of $1.75. The number of contracts is therefore

$$\frac{\$16,624}{\$1.75 \times 100} = 95$$

5. As shown in the example, the market value of the stock portfolio is equal to about 36 OEX contracts. If fewer than 36 contracts were written, the maximum value of the stock portfolio would be theoretically unlimited. Writing 36 or more contracts puts a limit on the portfolio price appreciation, with the limit occurring at the option striking price.

The index can rise from 298.96 to 315.00 (a rise of 5.36%) before the options become in-the-money. Therefore, the maximum value of the equity portfolio is

$$(\$996,975 \times 1.0536) + \$3,025 = \$1,053,438$$
$$\text{(stock)} \qquad\qquad \text{(cash)}$$

This assumes the option premium income was spent.

6. a. <u>10% rise</u>

stock:	$996,975 x 0.10 x 1.08 =	107,673 gain
calls:	100 x 56 x ($3.40 - 20.68) =	96,768 loss
	net	$10,905 gain

$996,975 + 10,905 + 3,025 = $1,010,905

   b. <u>10% decline</u>

stock:	$996,975 x -0.10 x 1.08 =	107,673 loss
calls:	100 x 56 x ($3.40 - 0) =	19,040 gain
	net	$ 88,633 loss

$996,975 - 88,633 + 3,025 = $911,367

7 - 9. Omitted

10.

	Calls			Puts		
	NOV	DEC	MAR	NOV	DEC	MAR
96	.941	.865	.754	-.055	-.127	-.226
98	.784	.711	.635	-.212	-.281	-.345
100	.503	.503	.501	-.493	-.489	-.479
102	.224	.298	.369	-.772	-.694	-.611

11. At-the-money futures puts and calls should sell for the same price. Therefore, the put should also sell for $2.

12.   With a striking price of 99, an underlying asset price of 100, a riskfree interest rate of 5%, a call premium of $2, and one-twelfth of a year until expiration, use the futures put-call parity relationship:

$$P = C - e^{-RT}(F-K)$$

$$= \$2 - e^{(.05)(1/12)}(\$100 - 99)$$

$$= \$1.00$$

Chapter Twenty-Three

Contemporary Issues in Portfolio Management

KEY POINTS

The book ends with a discussion of several "hot topics" in the portfolio management business. Tactical Asset Allocation, while generally conflicting with the efficient market hypothesis, is in vogue among investment practitioners, and all managers should know something about the technique.

Stock lending is an obscure part of the institutional money management business. The practice is both lucrative and full of potential for abuse. Increased regulatory supervision of this activity has already begun.

Long/short portfolios, like TAA, also seem to go against market efficiency. Still, they are actively pursued by many investment houses. The creation and transfer of stock certificates is increasingly expensive. There is a trend in the industry eventually to eliminate stock certificates, maintaining accounts in book entry form only.

Program trading continues to suffer from a bad image, largely due to a public misperception of what the term means and the effects of the practice.

TEACHING CONSIDERATIONS

As with any discipline, you cannot read a book and know it all. Students should appreciate the fact that the field of finance is continually evolving as increasingly sophisticated security analysts and portfolio managers search for ways to earn additional return and reduce risk.

It is particularly important for students to be able to evaluate any new investment strategy within the context of the efficient market hypothesis. Despite how someone feels about market efficiency, the implications of market efficiency upon an investment scheme should be clear. TAA is an excellent example of how a clairvoyant person can exploit market cycles. The problem is that few of us are clairvoyant and it is unlikely that many managers who actively seek to time the market will outperform a buy-and-hold strategy.

ANSWERS TO QUESTIONS

1. We do not expect to find riskless profits in a well-functioning marketplace. Securities are priced based on their expected returns and their perceived level of risk. Security valuation is, therefore, based on arbitrage arguments. Investments which dominate others will be preferred in the marketplace. It is the activities of security analysts and individual investors who eliminate arbitrage.

2. Increased volatility in the market is generally considered undesirable. A clear cause and effect would likely lead to calls for regulatory relief from program trading. Whether this would happen is a matter of conjecture.

3. If the market is efficient, no one can consistently time the market, and TAA strategies should be ineffective.

4. Asset class appraisal refers to an investigation of the relative merits of the various groups of securities into which an investment might be made.

5. With any active portfolio management strategy there is the potential that the active management might reduce returns rather than augment them. Failure to do at least as well as the market average is usually viewed as substandard managerial performance.

6. TAA can be consistent with any portfolio strategy that employs both fixed income securities and common stock. TAA is most commonly associated with an equity portfolio where capital appreciation is the primary objective.

7. You could switch between the long and short end of the yield curve, but this would be unusual. TAA is not normally associated with a fixed income portfolio.

8. Portfolio insurance requires alterations to the portfolio based on something that has already happened rather than on something that is expected to happen.

9. Selling short involves a potentially unlimited loss. Because of this "high risk," most brokerage firms discourage small investors from doing so.

10. Most individual investors are only concerned with the security of their investment, its potential return and risk, and with their ability to trade out of it at will. Whether stock is lent is generally unimportant.

11. They have usually not been given permission by the security owner.

12. Facilitating the matching up of those who want to lend stock and those who want to borrow it.

13. It is essentially "free money." There is no particular increase in risk, and it generates a reliable return. Only if one party defaults is there added risk.

14. What is the actual incidence of stock lending? Do some firms do more of this as a percentage of their assets than others? What rates of interest are paid, and how does this vary? What evidence is there that interest is ever credited to a customer account? What evidence is there that securities held in a cash account are sometimes lent?

15. Omitted.

16. Program trading seeks to eliminate arbitrage opportunities as they develop. Without arbitrage, program trading would be much less attractive.

17. A derivative asset is one whose value stems largely from the value of another asset. Calls, puts, and futures contracts are common examples.

18. Unless there is incremental benefit from the TAA program, the TAA manager can be accused of generating unnecessary commissions, which is not in the customer's best interest.

ANSWERS TO PROBLEMS

1.   Omitted.

2.   a.   1,000 x (1.0) + (10 x 100 x -0.317) = 683   (equivalent to a long position of 683 shares)

     b.   Sell short 317 shares.

3.   Omitted.

4.   Omitted.

Portfolio Construction, Management and Protection

TEST BANK

Chapter One

The Process of Portfolio Management

B. 1. Classical security analysis is sometimes called

    a. ABC analysis
    b. EIC analysis
    c. GBY analysis
    d. CPI analysis

C 2. The modern trend in investments is to _____ security analysis and _____ portfolio management.

    a. emphasize, emphasize
    b. emphasize, de-emphasize
    c. de-emphasize, emphasize
    d. de-emphasize, de-emphasize

B 3. Portfolio management is primarily concerned with

    a. increasing return
    b. reducing risk
    c. predicting the future
    d. explaining the past

D 4. Most of the academic literature of the past two decades has supported the

    a. arbitrage pricing theory
    b. benefits of high PE stocks
    c. usefulness of stock charts
    d. efficient markets paradigm

A 5. "The lower the dispersion in returns, the greater the accumulated value of otherwise equal investments." This statement is

    a. true
    b. false
    c. true for the short run, but not necessarily true for the long run
    d. true for the long run, but not necessarily true for the short run

D   6. _____ is cheap in the investment business.

       a. risk
       b. return
       c. time
       d. talk

A   7. Which of the following is a key concept in finance?

       a. A dollar today is worth more than a dollar tomor-
           row.
       b. Regardless of anything else, the higher the stock
           price, the better
       c. Regardless of anything else, the lower the risk,
           the better
       d. Risk averse people will not take a risk

B   8. Understanding _____ is essential to modern portfo-
       lio management.

       a. convexity
       b. duration
       c. semi-variance
       d. bond betas

C   9. According to the book, the first step in portfolio
       management is

       a. setting portfolio objectives
       b. formulating an investment strategy
       c. learning the basic principles of finance
       d. having a game plan for portfolio revision

B   10. A portfolio should have both _____ and _____
       objective.

       a. a short term, a long term
       b. a primary, a secondary
       c. an initial, a final
       d. an explicit, an implicit

A   11. One of the most consequential bits of academic
       research regarding portfolio construction is a paper by

       a. Evans and Archer
       b. Andrew and McLaughlin
       c. Lawrence and Philippatos
       d. Miles and Ezzell

B   12. _____ is a topic unique to this textbook.

      a. Real estate
      b. Security screening
      c. Performance evaluation
      d. Principles of the futures market

C   13. Real assets discussed in this book include

      a. art
      b. rare coins
      c. timberland
      d. diamonds

D   14. Which of the following is a popular means of in-
      creasing income from a portfolio?

      a. Selling bonds
      b. Selling stock short
      c. Buying put options
      d. Option overwriting

A   15. Portfolio protection was called _____ until the
      stock market crash in 1987.

      a. portfolio insurance
      b. portfolio hedging
      c. dynamic hedging
      d. arbitrage

D   16. In this text, the chapter on contemporary issues
      includes all of the following except

      a. tactical asset allocation
      b. stock lending
      c. program trading
      d. put-call parity

Chapter Two

The Two Key Concepts in Finance

B   1. A _____ value is the discounted value of one or more
    _____ cash flows.

   a. present, present
   b. present, future
   c. future, present
   d. future, future

D   2. If $1,000 is invested in a 2-year, 8% certificate of
    deposit, how much will be received at maturity?

   a. $1,155.78
   b. $1,178.65
   c. $1,145.98
   d. $1,166.40

D   3. If $1,000 is invested in a 2-year, 7% certificate of
    deposit, how much will be received at maturity?

   a. $1,055.72
   b. $1,275.65
   c. $1,045.18
   d. $1,144.90

A   4. An ordinary annuity is a _____ series of _____ cash
    flows.

   a. finite, constant
   b. finite, growing
   c. infinite, constant
   d. infinite, growing

B   5. The winner of a state lottery usually receives

   a. an ordinary annuity
   b. an annuity due
   c. a growing annuity
   d. a perpetuity

C   6. An annuity due is worth _____ than an ordinary
        annuity with the same number of payments.

        a. less
        b. the same as
        c. more
        d. no more than

A   7. You deposit $1,000 in a savings account which pays
        5% per year, compounded semi-annually. What is the
        account balance after two years?

        a. $1,103.81
        b. $1,116.98
        c. $1,145.92
        d. $1,188.02

B   8. You deposit $1,000 in a savings account which pays 5%
        per year, compounded quarterly. What is the account
        balance after two years?

        a. $1,100.00
        b. $1,104.49
        c. $1,125.66
        d. $1,198.22

B   9. If interest is compounded, the ____ yield will _____
        the _____ yield.

        a. effective, be less than, nominal
        b. effective, exceed, nominal
        c. nominal, exceed, effective
        d. nominal, equal, effective

A   10. Which of the following is the correct equation for
        determining a future value with continuous compounding?

        a. $PV \times e^{it} = FV$
        b. $PV \div e^{it} = FV$
        c. $PV \times e_{it} = FV$
        d. $PV \div e_{it} = FV$

B   11. Using a discount rate of 8% per year, what is the
       present value of an ordinary annuity of $100 per year
       for 10 years?

            a. $1,000
            b. $671
            c. $887
            d. $557

A   12. Using a discount rate of 8% per year, what is the
       present value of an annuity due of $100 per year with
       10 payments?

            a. $725
            b. $559
            c. $793
            d. $772

D   13. Using a discount rate of 8% per year (compounded
       quarterly), what is the present value of an ordinary
       annuity of $100 per year for 10 years?

            a. $726
            b. $662
            c. $811
            d. $684

C   14. A perpetual cash flow stream makes its first pay-
       ment of $500 in one year. Using a 7% annual discount
       rate and a 3% growth rate in the value of subsequent
       payments, what is the present value of this growing
       perpetuity?

            a. $2,000
            b. $20,000
            c. $12,500
            d. $125,000

B   15. A perpetuity makes annual payments of $250. The
       perpetuity is valued using a 10% discount rate. What
       is the value of the perpetuity if the first payment is
       made immediately?

            a. $2,500
            b. $2,750
            c. $25,000
            d. $2,525

A   16. The fact that most investors are risk averse means

            a. they will only take risks for which they are
                properly rewarded
            b. they will not take a risk
            c. they will not voluntarily take a risk
            d. they will not take a risk unless they know the
                outcome in advance

B   17. Which of the following statements is true?

            a. Everyone is risk averse.
            b. Some people are more risk averse than others.
            c. Risk averse people will not take a risk.
            d. Risk averse people are willing to settle for less
                return than risk neutral people

A   18. Risk must involve

            a. a chance of loss
            b. an unknown probability distribution
            c. actual dollars
            d. negative expected returns

C   19. Overall variability of returns is called

            a. systematic risk
            b. unsystematic risk
            c. total risk
            d. undiversifiable risk

B   20. Risk is often measured as

            a. central tendency of returns
            b. dispersion of returns
            c. expected value of returns
            d. possibility of negative returns

A   21. Riskier securities have _____ returns.

            a. higher expected
            b. lower realized
            c. higher instantaneous
            d. lower long-term

B   22. The market rewards investors for bearing _____
     risk.

          a. diversifiable
          b. undiversifiable
          c. unsystematic
          d. total

B   23. The diminishing marginal utility of money explains

          a. why some stocks sell for more than others
          b. why most people will not take a fair bet
          c. why people view the stock market as risky
          d. why people tend to pay too much

C   24. The text described an example of the diminishing
     marginal utility of money with a statement made by a
     _____ player.

          a. hockey
          b. football
          c. tennis
          d. basketball

C   25. Individual investment behavior is more a function
     of _____ than _____.

          a. risk, expected return
          b. expected return, utility
          c. utility, expected return
          d. expected return, risk

B   26. The St. Petersburg paradox explains

          a. why some stocks sell for more than others
          b. why most people will not take a fair bet
          c. why people view the stock market as risky
          d. why people tend to pay too much

A   27. In economic theory, if money is not saved, it is

          a. consumed
          b. invested
          c. unrealized
          d. deferred

D   28.   Wearing a Rolex watch is an example of someone
      getting

      a.   psychic return
      b.   utility
      c.   satisfaction
      d.   all of the above

B   29.   Two large classes of risk are

      a.   systematic and undiversifiable
      b.   price and convenience
      c.   realized and psychic
      d.   market and intermarket

C   30.   Individual consumption decisions are a major factor
      in determining

      a.   credit ratings of corporations
      b.   dividend rates
      c.   market interest rates
      d.   levels of perceived risk

Chapter Three

A Review of Statistical Principles Useful in Finance

B   1.   The holding period return is calculated as

   a. $(P_1 - P_0)/P_0$
   b. $(P_1 - P_0 + Income)/P_0$
   c. $(P_0 - P_1 + income)/P_0$
   d. $(P_1 - P_0 - income)/P_0$

C   2.   You bought 100 shares of stock at $35, received $3 per share in dividends, and sold the shares for $50. Your holding period return is

   a.   36%
   b. $1,503
   c.   51.4%
   d. $5,300

B   3.   Which of the following is true of the holding period return?

   a.   It considers the time value of money
   b.   It is independent of the passage of time
   c.   It explicitly considers risk
   d.   It only considers capital gains or losses

C   4.   A holding period return should only be compared with returns calculated:

   a.   over shorter periods
   b.   over longer periods
   c.   over periods of the same length
   d.   over periods of the same length or less

D   5.   A stock's return is 15.5%. The return relative is

   a.   0.845
   b.   -0.845
   c.   0.155
   d.   1.155

D   6. Return relatives are calculated primarily to deal
        with the potential problem of

            a.   changing returns
            b.   large returns
            c.   zero returns
            d.   negative returns

A   7. A stock has monthly returns of 4%, 5%, 2%, and -3%.
        Its arithmetic average return is

            a.   2%
            b.   3%
            c.   4%
            d.   5%

A   8. A stock has monthly returns of 4%, 5%, 2%, and -3%.
        Its geometric average return is

            a.   1.9%
            b.   2.1%
            c.   3.3%
            d.   cannot be determined

B   9. You buy a stock for $50 per share. Over the next
        four months, it has monthly returns of 4%, 5%, 2%, and
        -3%.   The value of a share at the end of the fourth
        month is

            a. $51.20
            b. $54.02
            c. $54.12
            d. $56.45

A   10. Suppose a stock pays no dividends. Another method
        of calculating the return relative is

            a. P_1/P_0
            b. P_0/P_1
            c. $(P_1-P_0)/P_0$
            d. $(P_0-P_1)/P_1$

A   11.   The arithmetic mean is always _____ the geometric
     mean.

          a.   greater than or equal to
          b.   greater than
          c.   less than or equal to
          d.   less than

A   12.   The _____ the dispersion in a series of numbers,
     the _____ the gap between the arithmetic and geometric
     mean.

          a.   greater, greater
          b.   greater, smaller
          c.   smaller, greater
          d.   more predictable, less predictable

A   13. Technically, _____ refers to the past; _____ refers
     to the future.

          a.   return, expected return
          b.   realized return, return
          c.   return relative, return
          d.   return, return relative

C   14.   According to the book, which of the following terms
     can mean different things to different people?

          a.   return on assets
          b.   return on equity
          c.   return on investment
          d.   return of principal

B   15.   The use of _____ can dramatically affect an inves-
     tor's return.

          a.   historical data
          b.   leverage
          c.   arithmetic averages
          d.   variance calculations

D   16.   Total risk can be measured by all of the following
       except

       a.   variance
       b.   standard deviation
       c.   semi-variance
       d.   arithmetic mean

D   17.   Var $(\tilde{x})$ = 25.   What is var $(2\tilde{x})$?

       a.   25
       b.   50
       c.   75
       d.   100

B   18.   Semi-variance only considers

       a.   extreme variation
       b.   adverse variation
       c.   unexpected variation
       d.   anticipated variation

C   19.   Discrete random variables are _____; continuous
       random variables are _____.

       a.   quantifiable, unquantifiable
       b.   objective, subjective
       c.   counted, measured
       d.   dependent, independent

B   20.   A variable whose value is based on the value of
       other variables is

       a.   an independent variable
       b.   a dependent variable
       c.   a stochastic variable
       d.   an estimated variable

A   21.   Random variables reside in a

       a.   population
       b.   sample
       c.   continuous set
       d.   discrete set

A   22. A jar contains a mixture of coins; you need a
quarter. From your perspective, the distribution of
coins in the jar is

    a. univariate
    b. bivariate
    c. trivariate
    d. multivariate

D   23. If a distribution shows more possible outcomes on
one side of the mean than the other, the distribution
shows

    a. uniformity
    b. normal characteristics
    c. random characteristics
    d. skewness

D   24. A coin-flipping experiment in which you measure
heads or tails takes observations from a _____ distri
bution.

    a. chi-square
    b. exponential
    c. Poisson
    d. binomial

D   25. Which of the following is a measure of central
tendency?

    a. skewness
    b. variance
    c. kurtosis
    d. mean

D   26.   The expected value of a random variable is also
called the

    a. skewness
    b. variance
    c. kurtosis
    d. mean

D   27.   A jar contains 100 quarters, 50 dimes, and 50
nickels.   What is the expected value of a single observation from this coin population?

       a. $0.375
       b. $0.200
       c. $0.133
       d. $0.163

D   28.   Which of the following can help reduce the effect
of outliers?

       a.   rounding
       b.   regression
       c.   interpolation
       d.   logarithms

C   29.   The expected value of $\tilde{x}$ is 5%.   What is $E(6\tilde{x})$?

       a.   0.833%
       b.   5%
       c.   30%
       d.   cannot be determined

A   30.   The correlation coefficient is equal to

       a. $COV(\tilde{a}, \tilde{b})/(\sigma_a\sigma_b)$
       b. $COV(\tilde{a}, \tilde{b})(\sigma_a)(\sigma_b)$
       c. $COV(\tilde{a}, \tilde{b})*\sigma_a/\sigma_b$
       d. $1 - [COV(\tilde{a}, \tilde{b})/(\sigma_a\sigma_b]$

A   31.   The minimum value of the correlation coefficient is

       a.   -1
       b.   0
       c.   +1
       d.   there is no minimum value

D   32.   The minimum value of covariance is

       a.   -1
       b.   0
       c.   +1
       d.   there is no minimum value

A   33. R squared is a measure of

      a. goodness of fit
      b. partial dispersion
      c. central tendency
      d. skewness

B   34. A sample of 100 observations has a standard devia-
      tion of 25. What is the standard error?

      a. 5
      b. 2.5
      c. .25
      d. cannot be determined

C   35. A sample of 100 observations has a standard devia-
      tion of 25 and a mean of 75. What is the 95% confidence
      interval?

      a. $50 \leq \tilde{x} \leq 75$
      b. $73 \leq \tilde{x} \leq 77$
      c. $70 \leq \tilde{x} \leq 80$
      d. $74.5 \leq \tilde{x} \leq 75.5$

B   36. $E(\tilde{R}_A) = 12\%$; $E(\tilde{R}_B) = 15\%$. What is the expected
      return of a portfolio which contains one third A and
      the remainder B?

      a. 12%
      b. 14%
      c. 15%
      d. 13.5%

A   37. A tilde ($\tilde{}$) over a symbol indicates it is a

      a. random variable
      b. constant
      c. continuous random variable
      d. discrete random variable

B   38. If two securities are negatively correlated, their
      covariance is

      a. positive
      b. negative
      c. zero
      d. cannot be determined

C   39.   The covariance between a random variable and a
               constant is

         a.   negative
         b.   positive
         c.   zero
         d.   non-negative

A   40. Return is

         a.   the benefit associated with an investment
         b.   the realized gain from an investment
         c.   the realized and unrealized gain from an invest-
               ment
         d.   the measurable gain from an investment

Chapter Four

Bond Prices and the Importance of Duration

D   1.   Bonds are identified by all of the following except

    a.   issuer
    b.   maturity
    c.   coupon
    d.   rating

B   2.   How much interest does an XYZ 7s09 bond pay each year?

    a.   9% of par
    b.   7% of par
    c.   7.09% of par
    d.   cannot be determined

B   3.   The details of a bond issue are contained in the

    a.   debenture
    b.   indenture
    c.   confirmation statement
    d.   call agreement

A   4.   U. S. treasury bonds are _____ issues.

    a.   full faith and credit
    b.   secured
    c.   subordinated
    d.   corporate

B   5.   Which of the following is the correct order of increasing maturity?

    a.   bills, bonds, notes
    b.   bills, notes, bonds
    c.   notes, bills, bonds
    d.   notes, bonds, bills

C   6.   Which of the following are most similar?

    a.   bills and notes
    b.   bills and bonds
    c.   notes and bonds
    d.   they are all equally similar

B   7. A debenture is like a _____ loan.

      a. secured
      b. signature
      c. automobile
      d. mortgage

A   8. Which of the following is most likely to be financed
      by a revenue bond?

      a. bridge
      b. low-income housing complex
      c. fleet of corporate automobiles
      d. airplane

B   9. Treasury bonds have an initial life of more than ___
      years.

      a. five
      b. ten
      c. fifteen
      d. twenty

C   10. A debt which uses land and buildings as collateral
      is a _____ loan.

      a. collateral trust
      b. equipment trust
      c. mortgage
      d. senior

C   11. A cash reserve for the ultimate repayment of bond
      principal is a

      a. reserve fund
      b. depreciation fund
      c. sinking fund
      d. interest-only fund

B   12. A fleet of trucks might logically be financed with

      a. collateral trust bonds
      b. equipment trust certificates
      c. mortgages
      d. treasury bonds

A   13.   A loan with a large final payment is a _____ loan.

    a.   balloon
    b.   escrow
    c.   inflated
    d.   descending

B   14.   A bond on which the interest is payable only if it is earned is a(n) _____ bond.

    a.   sinking fund
    b.   income
    c.   subordinated
    d.   full faith and credit

C   15.   An income bond is most likely to be associated with financing which of the following?

    a.   an apartment complex
    b.   a public highway
    c.   a toll bridge
    d.   capital improvements to a park

B   16.   Typical bond cash flows include all of the following except

    a.   annuity plus lump sum
    b.   growing annuity plus lump sum
    c.   perpetuity
    d.   lump sum only

C   17.   An example of a variable rate security is a

    a.   fixed rate mortgage
    b.   consol
    c.   U. S. savings bond
    d.   zero coupon bond

B   18.   A famous commodity-backed convertible bond was issued by a _____ company.

    a.   soybean processing
    b.   silver mining
    c.   sugar refining
    d.   savings and loan

C   19. New debt may no longer be issued in _____ form.

       a.   book entry
       b.   registered
       c.   bearer
       d.   convertible

B   20. If you hold a bond certificate with your name on it, it is a _____ bond.

       a.   book entry
       b.   registered
       c.   bearer
       d.   convertible

A   21. Newly issued bonds issued by the U. S. Treasury are in _____ form only.

       a.   book entry
       b.   registered
       c.   bearer
       d.   convertible

C   22. An individual who wishes to buy a U. S. Treasury bond must open an account through the

       a.   Federal Reserve System
       b.   Security Investor Protection Corporation
       c.   Treasury Direct System
       d.   Federal Deposit Insurance Corporation

C   23. The clipping of coupons is associated with _____ bonds.

       a.   book entry
       b.   registered
       c.   bearer
       d.   convertible

A   24. To solve for a bond's yield to maturity with semi-
     annual interest payments,

          a.   divide the discount rate by two and double the
                number of periods
          b.   divide the discount rate by two and halve the
                number of periods
          c.   multiply the discount rate by two and double the
                number of periods
          d.   multiply the discount rate by two and halve the
                number of periods

C   25. You own $5,000 par of the XYZ 8s of 99. The bond
     paid interest six months ago, and pays again tomorrow.
     How much is the next interest check?

          a. $40
          b. $80
          c. $200
          d. $400

C   26. You own $5,000 par of the XYZ 8s of 99; they sell
     for 94% of par. The bond paid interest six months ago,
     and pays again tomorrow. How much is the next interest
     check?

          a. $376
          b. $188
          c. $200
          d. $400

C   27. A consol is valued as a

          a. level annuity
          b. annuity due
          c. perpetuity
          d. growing perpetuity

B   28. The quantity $\sum_{t=1}^{\infty} \dfrac{C}{(1+R)^t}$ equals

          a. C x R
          b. C ÷ R
          c. C^R
          d. R^C

C   29. What is the value of a consol which pays $100 per year if the required rate of return is 8%?

    a. $800
    b. $1000
    c. $1250
    d. $1500

A   30. The yield to maturity calculation assumes that _____ are reinvested at the yield to maturity.

    a. coupon proceeds
    b. sinking fund payments
    c. the principal payments
    d. dollars equal to the purchase price

D   31. A specific yield to maturity can only be locked in with which of the following bonds?

    a. consol
    b. variable rate
    c. convertible
    d. zero coupon

C   32. The effective annual rate is also called the

    a. arithmetic mean return
    b. geometric mean return
    c. realized compound yield
    d. internal rate of return

C   33. If a bond sells for par,

    a. current yield exceeds the yield to maturity
    b. current yield is less than the yield to maturity
    c. current yield equals yield to maturity
    d. none of the above

A   34. If a bond sells at a premium,

    a. current yield exceeds the yield to maturity
    b. current yield is less than the yield to maturity
    c. current yield equals yield to maturity
    d. none of the above

B   35.   If a bond sells at a discount,

    a.   current yield exceeds the yield to maturity
    b.   current yield is less than the yield to maturity
    c.   current yield equals yield to maturity
    d.   none of the above

A   36.   If a bond sells at a premium,

    a.   its price must decline over time
    b.   its price must rise over time
    c.   its price will remain relatively constant over time
    d.   its price will be very volatile over time

D   37.   Someone who relies on investment income for living expenses is most concerned with

    a.   internal rate of return
    b.   yield to maturity
    c.   realized compound yield
    d.   current yield

C   38.   The yield curve is normally

    a.   flat
    b.   descending
    c.   upward sloping
    d.   none of the above

B   39.   The yield curve normally has a _____ first derivative and a _____ second derivative.

    a.   positive, positive
    b.   positive, negative
    c.   negative, positive
    d.   negative, negative

A   40.   If all interest rates rise by a similar amount, this is a _____ in the yield curve.

    a.   parallel shift
    b.   stochastic aberration
    c.   non-parallel shift
    d.   non-stochastic aberration

B   41.   Corporate bonds rated BBB will show a _____ of
        yield curve than U. S. Treasury bonds.

            a.   lower level
            b.   higher level
            c.   flatter plot
            d.   steeper plot

B   42. Forward interest rates are mostly associated with
        the _____ theory of interest rate structure.

            a.   liquidity premium
            b.   expectations
            c.   inflation premium
            d.   normal backwardation

B   43.   Two year certificates of deposit yield 5.00%; a
        one-year CD has a 4.66% rate. What is the one year
        forward rate?

            a.   4.66%
            b.   5.34%
            c.   5.66%
            d.   5.77%

B   44.   If the expectations theory of interest rates is
        accurate, the only explanation for an upward sloping
        yield curve is

            a.   fear of inflation
            b.   an expectation that interest rates will continu-
                 ally increase
            c.   demand for liquidity
            d.   risk aversion

A   45. According to the liquidity premium theory of inter-
        est rates,

            a.   forward rates are actually higher than the ex-
                  pected interest rate
            b.   forward rates are actually lower than the ex-
                  pected interest rate
            c.   forward rates are equal to the expected interest
                  rate
            d.   none of the above

B   46.   A $1000 par bond has a conversion price of $33.50.
Its conversion ratio is

        a. $29.85
        b.   29.85 shares
        c. $33,500
        d.   33,500 shares

C   47. A $1000 par bond sells for $900 and has a conversion ratio of 25 shares. If the underlying stock price
is $35, the conversion value is

        a. $25
        b. $100
        c. $875
        d. $935

B   48.   A bond's ____ should never be _____ than its _____.

        a.   conversion value, less, market value
        b.   conversion value, more, market value
        c.   conversion ratio, less, conversion price
        d.   conversion price, less, conversion ratio

A   49.   The maximum level of accrued interest with most
bonds occurs _____ times a year.

        a.   two
        b.   four
        c.   six
        d.   twelve

A   50.   The amount a bond buyer pays is

        a.   principal + accrued interest + brokerage fees
        b.   principal - accrued interest + brokerage fees
        c.   accrued interest - principal + brokerage fees
        d.   accrued interest - principal - brokerage fees

C   51.   How much interest has accrued on an 8%, $1000 par
bond seven days after the last interest payment date?

        a.   none
        b. $1.00
        c. $1.53
        d. $40.00

C   52.   Credit risk is also called

       a.   interest rate risk
       b.   purchasing power risk
       c.   default risk
       d.   reinvestment rate risk

C   53.   Standard & Poor's bond ratings measure

       a.   interest rate risk
       b.   purchasing power risk
       c.   default risk
       d.   reinvestment rate risk

C   54.   The demarcation between investment grade bonds and
       junk bonds is the S&P _____ rating.

       a.   AAA
       b.   AA
       c.   BBB
       d.   B

A   55.   _____ is a leading bond rating service.

       a.   Moody's Investors Service
       b.   Weissenberger's Investment Service
       c.   Value Line Investment Survey
       d.   Morningstar

A   56.   The fact that bond prices change as market interest
       rates change is a result of

       a.   interest rate risk
       b.   purchasing power risk
       c.   default risk
       d.   reinvestment rate risk

A   57.   Which of the following has no interest rate risk?

       a.   non-negotiable certificate of deposit
       b.   U. S. Treasury bond
       c.   corporate bond
       d.   mortgage

A   58. Call risk is a type of _____ risk.

    a. convenience
    b. market
    c. interest rate
    d. default

D   59. If a bond is called, the bondholder often receives

    a. less than the par value
    b. the par value minus the last coupon payment
    c.   the par value minus the last year's coupon pay-
         ment
    d. the par value plus a call premium

C   60. The _____ the _____ on a bond, the higher its
         reinvestment rate risk.

    a. higher, yield to maturity
    b. lower, yield to maturity
    c. higher, coupon
    d. lower, coupon

C   61. Marketability risk refers to

    a. the possibility of selling a bond for less than
        the price paid
    b. the possibility of having the bond called
    c. the difficulty in selling a bond
    d. the magnitude of the total bond risk

B   62. Bond prices move _____ with market yields.

    a. directly
    b. inversely
    c. exponentially
    d. logarithmically

D   63. A famous set of bond pricing relationships is

    a. Kondradiev's theorems
    b. the Dow theory
    c. Fibonacci theorems
    d. Malkiel's theorems

B   64. _____ term bonds have more _____ risk.

      a.   Longer, reinvestment rate
      b.   Longer, interest rate
      c.   Shorter, reinvestment rate
      d.   Shorter, interest rate

A   65. _____ coupon bonds have more _____ risk.

      a.   Higher, reinvestment rate
      b.   Higher, interest rate
      c.   Lower, reinvestment rate
      d.   Lower, interest rate

D   66. If interest rates fall, $\blacktriangle_t$ is the price change in a bond with "t" years until maturity. Suppose there are four bonds: $\blacktriangle_2$, $\blacktriangle_4$, $\blacktriangle_{22}$, $\blacktriangle_{24}$. If the bonds are identical in every respect except for their maturity, which of the following statements is true?

      a. $(\blacktriangle_2 - \blacktriangle_4) > 0$
      b. $(\blacktriangle_2 - \blacktriangle_4) = 0$
      c. $(\blacktriangle_2 - \blacktriangle_4) - (\blacktriangle_{22} - \blacktriangle_{24}) > 0$
      d. $(\blacktriangle_2 - \blacktriangle_4) - (\blacktriangle_{22} - \blacktriangle_{24}) < 0$

A   67. Malkiel's theorem five deals with

      a.   bond capital gains and losses
      b.   changing default risk levels
      c.   declining interest rates
      d.   call risk

B   68. The principal value of duration is the fact that

      a.   it makes knowledge of default risk unnecessary
      b.   it incorporates Malkiel's theorems in a single number
      c.   it incorporates default risk into interest rate risk
      d.   it eliminates the reinvestment rate risk problem

D   69. A definition of duration is

      a.   the weighted average life of a bond
      b.   the weighted average value of a bond's cash flows
      c.   the weighted average of the bond's marketability risk
      d.   the weighted average time until cash flows occur

A   70.   In calculating duration via the traditional method,
       the "weights" reflect

           a.   the time value of money
           b.   the level of default risk
           c.   the level of interest rate risk
           d.   the cost of capital

Chapter Five

Setting Portfolio Objectives

A   1.   Two dominant factors contributing to a successful investment program are

    a.   suitable investment objectives and policy, and successful managers

    b.   suitable investment objectives and risk assessment

    c.   successful managers and successful income generation

    d.   accurate risk assessment and measurement of historical return

B   2.   To an investment professional, which of the following provides no growth?

    a.   real estate

    b.   savings accounts

    c.   common stock

    d.   corporate bonds

B   3.   With bequests, a semantic problem sometimes develops with regard to the meaning of the terms

    a.   growth and income

    b.   principal and interest

    c.   risk and return

    d.   present value and future value

D   4.   A good example of the issue of multiple portfolio beneficiaries is found in

    a.   people who want income and those who want growth

    b.   people who are risk averse and those who are not

    c.   people who pay taxes and those who do not

    d.   people today and people tomorrow

A   5.   Which of the following deals with decisions that
     have been made about long-term investment activities,
     eligible investment categories, and the allocation of
     funds among the eligible investment categories?

          a.   investment policy
          b.   investment strategy
          c.   investment tactics
          d.   investment standards

C   6.   All of the following are principal portfolio objec-
     tives EXCEPT

          a.   stability of principal
          b.   capital appreciation
          c.   growth and income
          d.   income

A   7.   If someone wants no chance of a loss of principal
     value, the appropriate primary objective is

          a.   stability of principal
          b.   income
          c.   growth of income
          d.   capital appreciation

C   8.   If someone is concerned about inflation eroding
     purchasing power of regular income, the appropriate
     primary objective is

          a.   stability of principal
          b.   income
          c.   growth of income
          d.   capital appreciation

D   9.   A young, well-paid professional is best suited, on
     average, to which primary objective?

          a.   stability of principal
          b.   income
          c.   growth of income
          d.   capital appreciation

D   10. In the early years, which primary objective gener-
     ally results in the least income?

          a. stability of principal
          b. income
          c. growth of income
          d. capital appreciation

A   11. A growth-of-income objective

          a. sacrifices some current return for some purchas-
              ing power protection
          b. generates maximum income as soon as possible
          c. makes only sparing use of equity securities
          d. generates income that declines over time

B   12. Tax-free income can be earned by investing in

          a. corporate bonds
          b. municipal bonds
          c. Treasury bonds
          d. common stock

C   13. All investors seek to

          a. maximize their expected return
          b. minimize their risk exposure
          c. maximize their expected utility
          d. minimize the number of their capital losses

B   14. Some people do not like mutual funds because they

          a. have no tax advantages
          b. are not exciting
          c. offer less potential return than that available
              in securities
          d. are too risky

D   15. Establishing a secondary objective helps the port-
          folio manager

          a. learn more about the client's tax situation
          b. learn more about the client's expected utility of
              investment
          c. determine the appropriate level of risk for the
              customer
          d.   determine the necessary level of equity invest-
              ment

C   16. Which of the following primary/secondary objective
         combinations is infeasible?

         a.   stability of principal, income
         b.   income, stability of principal
         c.   growth of income, stability of principal
         d.   capital appreciation, growth of income

A   17. Which of the following primary/secondary objective
         combinations is infeasible?

         a.   stability of principal, growth of income
         b.   income, growth of income
         c.   growth of income, capital appreciation
         d.   income, capital appreciation

B   18. Which of the following primary/secondary objective
         combinations is infrequent?

         a.   stability of principal, growth of income
         b.   income, capital appreciation
         c.   growth of income, capital appreciation
         d.   growth of income, stability of principal

A   19. A disadvantage of portfolio splitting is that it

         a.   enables overseers to avoid making tough decisions
         b.   reduces current income
         c.   reduces the potential for capital appreciation
         d.   sacrifices liquidity

A   20. A common third category of investment (in addition
         to bonds and stock) is

         a.   cash equivalents
         b.   municipal securities
         c.   American depository receipts
         d.   repurchase agreements

A   21. Another name for portfolio dedication is

         a.   liability funding
         b.   technical analysis
         c.   fundamental analysis
         d.   strategic investment

B   22. Cash matching involves assembling a portfolio such
         that

         a. it has the duration desired
         b.   it has a cash flow stream that matches the re-
             quirements of a liability stream
         c. it optimizes the risk/return combination
         d. it is informationally efficient

A   23. Principal concerns in duration matching are

         a. the present value of the outflows and their
             duration
         b. the future value of the outflows and their dura-
             tion
         c. the annuity value of the outflows
         d. the certainty equivalent of the outflows and the
             present value of its duration

D   24. To reduce the duration of a bond portfolio, _____
         are often used.

         a. shares of common stock
         b. hard asset investments
         c. preferred stock shares
         d. treasury bills

C   25. The first mutual fund was founded in

         a. 1776
         b. 1815
         c. 1924
         d. 1957

C   26. The approximate number of mutual funds in the
         United States is

         a. 100
         b. 1,000
         c. 3,000
         d. 30,000

A   27. Which of the following trades on a stock exchange?

         a. a closed-end fund
         b. an open-end fund
         c. any mutual fund
         d. any investment company

C   28. For an open-end mutual fund,

            a. net asset value < market value
            b. net asset value > market value
            c. net asset value = market value
            d. net asset value is greater than or equal to
                market value

C   29. If you buy shares in a load fund, you will pay

            a. net asset value
            b. less than net asset value
            c. more than net asset value
            d. cannot be determined

A   30. Before buying mutual fund shares, prospective
            investors must receive a

            a. prospectus
            b. indenture
            c. debenture
            d. hypothecation agreement

Chapter Six

The Mathematics of Diversification

A   1.   The work of Harry Markowitz is based on the search for

        a.   efficient portfolios
        b.   undervalued securities
        c.   the highest long-term growth rates
        d.   minimum risk portfolios

B   2.   Securities A and B have expected returns of 12% and 15%, respectively. If you put 30% of your money in Security A and the remainder in B, what is the portfolio expected return?

        a.   13.4%
        b.   14.1%
        c.   14.6%
        d.   15.3%

D   3.   Securities A and B have expected returns of 12% and 15%, respectively. If you put 40% of your money in Security A and the remainder in B, what is the portfolio expected return?

        a.   13.4%
        b.   13.8%
        c.   14.6%
        d.   15.3%

B   4.   The variance of a 2-security portfolio decreases as the return correlation of the two securities

        a.   increases
        b.   decreases
        c.   changes in either direction
        d.   cannot be determined

D   5.   A security has a return variance of 25%. The standard deviation of returns is

        a.   5%
        b.   15%
        c.   25%
        d.   50%

C   6.   A security has a return variance of 16%. The standard deviation of returns is

    a.   4%
    b.   16%
    c.   40%
    d.   50%

A   7.   Covariance is the product of two security's

    a.   expected deviations from their means
    b.   standard deviations
    c.   betas
    d.   standard deviations divided by their correlation

C   8.   The covariance of a random variable with itself is

    a.   its correlation with itself
    b.   its standard deviation
    c.   its variance
    d.   equal to 1.0

D   9.   Covariance is _____; correlation is _____.

    a.   positive; positive or negative
    b.   negative; positive or negative
    c.   positive or negative; positive or zero
    d.   positive or negative, positive or negative

C   10. For a six security portfolio, it is necessary to
calculate ___ covariances plus ___ variances.

    a.   36,6
    b.   30,6
    c.   15,6
    d.   30,12

B   11. COV(A,B) = .335. What is COV(B,A)?

    a.   -0.335
    b.   0.335
    c.   (0.335 x 0.335)
    d.   cannot be determined

A   12. One of the first proponents of the single index
        model was

        a.   William Sharpe
        b.   Robert Merton
        c.   Eugene Fama
        d.   Merton Miller

B   13. Without knowing beta, determining portfolio vari-
        ance with a sixty security portfolio requires ___
        statistics per security.

        a.   1
        b.   60
        c.   3600/2
        d.   3600

B   14. Securities A, B, and C have betas of 1.2, 1.3, and
        1.7, respectively.   What is the beta of an equally
        weighted portfolio of all three?

        a.   1.15
        b.   1.40
        c.   1.55
        d.   1.60

B   15. Securities A, B, and C have betas of 1.2, 1.3, and
        1.7, respectively.   What is the beta of a portfolio
        composed of 1/2 A and 1/4 each of B and C?

        a.   1.15
        b.   1.35
        c.   1.55
        d.   1.60

B   16. A security has a beta of 1.2; the market variance
        is 0.25. What is the security's variance?

        a.   0.33
        b.   0.36
        c.   0.41
        d.   0.44

B   17. Security A has a beta of 1.2; security B has a beta
       of 0.8.   If the market variance is 0.30, what is
       COV(A,B)?

            a.   .255
            b.   .288
            c.   .314
            d.   .355

B   18. As portfolio size increases, the variance of the
       error term generally

            a.   increases
            b.   decreases
            c.   approaches 1.0
            d.   becomes erratic

C   19. The least risk two security portfolio is called the

            a.   optimum portfolio
            b.   efficient portfolio
            c.   minimum variance portfolio
            d.   market portfolio

B   20. Industry effects are associated with

            a.   the single index model
            b.   the multi-index model
            c.   the Markowitz model
            d.   the covariance matrix

A   21. COV(A,B) is equal to

            a.   the product of their standard deviations and
                 their correlation
            b.   the product of their variances and their correla-
                 tion
            c.   the product of their standard deviations and
                 their covariances
            d.   the product of their variances and their covari-
                 ances

A   22. The covariance between a constant and a random
        variable is

        a.   zero
        b.   1.0
        c.   their correlation
        d.   the product of their betas

D   23.   The covariance between a security's returns and
        those of the market index is 0.03. If the security
        beta is 1.15, what is the market variance?

        a.   0.005
        b.   0.010
        c.   0.021
        d.   0.026

D   24.   COV(A,B) = 0.50; the variance of the market is
        0.25, and the beta of Security A is 1.00. What is the
        beta of security B?

        a. 1.00
        b. 1.25
        c. 1.50
        d. 2.00

D   25.   There are 1,700 stocks in the Value Line index.
        How many covariances would have to be calculated in
        order to use the Markowitz full covariance model?

        a.   1,700
        b.   5,650
        c.   12,350
        d.   1,444,150

Chapter Seven

Why Diversification is a Good Idea

A   1. Risk averse people only take risks

    a. when they believe they will be rewarded for doing so
    b. when they have to
    c. when it is necessary to seek some additional return
    d. when actual returns are below expected return

C   2. The collection of eligible investments is called the

    a. eligible set
    b. efficient set
    c. security universe
    d. principal components

C   3. A security dominates another if

    a. it offers the same expected return with less risk
    b. it offers higher expected return for the same risk
    c. both a and b
    d. none of the above

B   4. In the absence of a riskfree rate, the minimum variance portfolio

    a. is usually efficient
    b. is always efficient
    c. is never efficient
    d. is unrelated to market efficiency

A   5. Portfolios that are not dominated

    a. lie on the efficient frontier
    b. are minimum risk portfolios
    c. have maximum expected returns
    d. have low correlations

A   6. With the availability of a riskfree rate, the effi
         cient frontier becomes

         a. linear
         b. curved
         c. jagged
         d. less attractive

C   7. Portfolios do not exist that lie

         a. at the far right of the efficient frontier
         b. at the far left of the efficient frontier
         c. above the efficient frontier
         d. below the efficient frontier

A   8. The line passing through the risk free rate and the
         market portfolio is called the

         a. capital market line
         b. optimum combination line
         c. dominant line
         d. unlevered investment line

C   9. According to the separation theorem, all investors
         should hold

         a. as many securities as possible
         b. as many uncorrelated securities as possible
         c. only the riskfree rate and the market portfolio
         d. only two risky portfolios on the efficient fron-
             tier

D   10. Efficient portfolios to the left of the market
         portfolio are called

         a. borrowing portfolios
         b. fully invested portfolios
         c. dominant portfolios
         d. lending portfolios

A   11. Most computer output of efficient portfolios lists
         only the

         a. corner portfolios
         b. odd-numbered portfolios
         c. low variance portfolios
         d. maximum return portfolios

D   12.   The Markowitz algorithm is an application of

        a.   linear programming
        b.   goal programming
        c.   integer programming
        d.   quadratic programming

Chapter Eight

The Capital Markets and Market Efficiency

B   1. Capital markets trade securities with

      a. a life of less than one year
      b. a life of more than one year
      c. a life of more than ten years
      d. a life of more than fifteen years

A   2. The most important function of the capital markets is the ___ function.

      a. economic
      b. continuous pricing
      c. fair price
      d. taxation

A   3. Which function of the capital markets facilitates the flow of capital from savers to borrowers?

      a. economic
      b. continuous pricing
      c. fair price
      d. taxation

B   4. Which function of the capital markets enables market participants to get accurate, up-to-date price information?

      a. economic
      b. continuous pricing
      c. fair price
      d. taxation

C   5. The _____ function of the capital markets removes the fear of buying or selling at an unreasonable price.

      a. economic
      b. continuous pricing
      c. fair price
      d. taxation

D   6. Fair pricing of securities is associated with

         a. the fair pricing theory
         b. the separation theorem
         c. the central limit theorem
         d. the efficient market hypothesis

A   7. The "efficiency" referred to in the efficient market
         hypothesis is _____ efficiency.

         a. informational
         b. operational
         c. taxation
         d. inflation adjusted

C   8. The weak form of the efficient market hypothesis
         states that _____ are of no use in predicting future
         stock prices.

         a. balance sheets
         b. earnings reports
         c. charts
         d. annual reports

D   9. People who employ charting techniques in the analy-
         sis of securities are called

         a. operational security analysts
         b. fundamental security analysts
         c. informational security analysts
         d. technical security analysts

D   10. To an investment professional, which of the follow-
         ing is most important?

         a. past prices
         b. past and present prices
         c. future prices
         d. present and future prices

A   11. A means of investigating the weak form of market
         efficiency is via a _____ test.

         a. runs
         b. charting
         c. subjective
         d. psychological

D   12.   How many runs are in the following sequence?

HHHTTTHTHTHHHTTH

    a.   6
    b.   7
    c.   8
    d.   9

B   13. The _____ form of the efficient market hypothesis states that security prices fully reflect all relevant publicly available information.

    a.   weak
    b.   semi-strong
    c.   strong
    d.   semi-efficient

B   14. Tests regarding stock splits or dividends are usually tests of the _____ form of market efficiency.

    a.   weak
    b.   semi-strong
    c.   strong
    d.   semi-efficient

C   15. Inside information is associated with the ____ form of market efficiency.

    a.   weak
    b.   semi-strong
    c.   strong
    d.   semi-efficient

D   16. The notion that some stocks are priced more effi ciently than others is associated with the

    a.   weak form of the EMH
    b.   semi-strong form of the EMH
    c.   strong form of the EMH
    d.   semi-efficient market hypothesis

D   17. The random walk idea says that

    a.   stock prices move randomly
    b.   interest rates change randomly
    c.   the stock market averages change randomly
    d.   the news arrives randomly

A   18.   In finance, the term _____ is associated with an
       unexplained   result that deviates from that expected by
       finance theory.

          a.   anomaly
          b.   paradigm
          c.   inefficiency
          d.   abnormal profit

B   19.   There is some evidence that ___ PE stocks outper
       form stocks with _____ PEs.

          a.   high, lower
          b.   low, higher
          c.   extreme, more normal
          d.   median, more unusual

A   20.   The small firm effect states that

          a.   firms with low capitalizations outperform larger
               firms
          b.   firms with high capitalizations outperform small-
               er firms
          c.   firms with average capitalizations outperform
               average size firms
          d.   firms with large or small capitalizations outper-
               form average size firms

A   21.   Stock returns are inexplicably high in

          a.   January
          b.   May
          c.   September
          d.   November

B   22.   A subfield of physics which is being applied to
       finance is

          a.   quantum mechanics
          b.   chaos theory
          c.   angular momentum
          d.   harmonic motion

B   23.   Which of the following is a Fibonacci number?

        a.   12
        b.   13
        c.   14
        d.   15

A   24.   An odd thing about Fibonacci numbers is

        a.   the frequency with which they appear in nature
        b.   their predictive ability
        c.   the fact that they are all even
        d.   the fact that they are all odd

B   25.   The first five Fibonacci numbers are 1, 1, 2, 3, 5.
What is the sixth?

        a.   6
        b.   8
        c.   12
        d.   cannot be determined

D   26.   Leonardo Fibonacci discovered the sequence of
numbers which bears his name while exploring

        a.   the stars
        b.   the behavior of ants
        c.   scores of dart contests
        d.   the reproduction rates of rabbits

Chapter Nine

International Investment and Diversification

D   1.   In 1989, pension fund investment overseas totaled about

      a. $250 million
      b. $ 1 billion
      c. $ 5 billion
      d. $20 billion

B   2.   When the Evans and Archer study is repeated with a security universe that includes international securities, the level of systematic risk

      a.   increases
      b.   decreases
      c.   remains unchanged
      d.   there is no relation between systematic risk and the Evans and Archer study

C   3.   For U. S. securities, market risk accounts for about ____ of a security's total risk.

      a.   5%
      b.   17%
      c.   27%
      d.   54%

B   4.   The correlation among securities on European exchanges is generally

      a.   decreasing
      b.   increasing
      c.   remaining unchanged
      d.   cannot be determined

D   5.   According to a study by Bruno Solnik, what percentage of total risk can be diversified away by holding international securities?

      a.   one half
      b.   five eighths
      c.   three fourths
      d.   seven eighths

C   6. Globally, the number of equity securities is about

          a. 100,000
          b. 250,000
          c. 1 million
          d. 100 million

A   7. The changing relationships among currencies of
          interest to you constitutes _____ risk.

          a. foreign exchange
          b. political
          c. social
          d. international

B   8. If something costs NZ$110 and the exchange rate
          between the New Zealand dollar and the U. S. dollar is
          $0.5855/NZ$, what is the cost in U. S. dollars?

          a. $58.55
          b. $64.41
          c. $110.00
          d. $187.88

B   9. Suppose someone holds a security denominated in
          Australian dollars. If the Australian value of the
          security does not change but the U. S. dollar depreci-
          ates relative to the Australian dollar, the security
          holder has a

          a. paper loss
          b. paper gain
          c. realized gain
          d. realized loss

A   10. A security was purchased for ¥10,000, when the
          exchange rate was ¥750/$. The security was later sold
          for ¥12,000 and the exchange rate had changed to
          ¥850/$. What was the holding period return from a US
          investor's perspective?

          a. -5.9%
          b. -2.3%
          c.   2.3%
          d.   5.9%

A   11.   An investor's exchange rate "frame of reference" is called the

    a.   currency of account
    b.   exchange rate
    c.   nominal rate
    d.   international standard

D   12.   The nominal rate of interest is a function of all of the following EXCEPT

    a.   real rate
    b.   inflation rate
    c.   risk premium
    d.   prime rate

C   13.   The current price of a foreign currency is the ___ rate.

    a.   forward
    b.   futures
    c.   spot
    d.   delivery

A   14.   The contractual rate between a bank and a client delivery for the future delivery of foreign exchange is the ___ rate.

    a.   forward
    b.   futures
    c.   spot
    d.   delivery

A   15.   A U. S. storekeeper who entered into an obligation to pay Swiss francs for a delivery of goods could hedge the foreign exchange risk by

    a.   entering into a forward contract to buy Swiss francs
    b.   entering into a forward contract to deliver Swiss francs
    c.   buying a foreign currency which is negatively correlated with the Swiss franc
    d.   buying a foreign currency which is positively correlated with the Swiss franc

A   16. Forward rate reflect differences in

     a. national interest rates
     b. risk premiums
     c. the time value of money
     d. tax treatment

B   17. Inflation in the home country causes the value of
     the home currency to _____ in the global market.

     a. appreciate
     b. depreciate
     c. fluctuate
     d. change

D   18. The text described an example of purchasing power
     parity using

     a. automobiles
     b. bottles of wine
     c. airline tickets
     d. Big Mac hamburgers

B   19. The extent to which you face foreign exchange risk
     is

     a. nominal risk
     b. exposure
     c. political risk
     d. arbitrage risk

Chapter Ten

Picking the Equity Players

A   1.   The three kinds of dividends firms pay are

     a.   stock, cash, and property
     b.   stock, special, and regular
     c.   cash, special, and regular
     d.   monthly, quarterly, and year-end

B   2.   Securities held on your behalf by a broker are

     a.   held in a margin account
     b.   held in a street name
     c.   registered in your name with the issuing company
     d.   ineligible for corporate dividends

D   3.   Which of the following is an odd lot?

     a.   100 shares
     b.   500 shares
     c.   11,000 shares
     d.   11,300 shares

C   4.   A spin-off is similar to a

     a.   stock split
     b.   stock dividend
     c.   property dividend
     d.   cash dividend

A   5.   Rights are associated with

     a.   new stock issues
     b.   new bond issues
     c.   any new security issue
     d.   newly incorporated firms

B   6.   The third date in the dividend payment chronology is

     a.   the date of declaration
     b.   the ex-dividend date
     c.   the date of record
     d.   the date of payment

B   7.   Stock prices tend to fall on

        a.   the date of declaration
        b.   the ex-dividend date
        c.   the date of record
        d.   the date of payment

B   8.   A company's date of record for a dividend is September 15. Which of the following is most likely to be the ex-dividend date?

        a.   September 1
        b.   September 11
        c.   September 19
        d.   October 1

A   9.   Dividend growth rates are of primary importance to

        a.   fundamental analysts
        b.   technical analysts
        c.   original analysts
        d.   chartists

B   10. A stock's current dividend is $4.56; ten years ago it was $2.88. What has been the average annual dividend growth rate?

        a.   4.0%
        b.   4.7%
        c.   5.6%
        d.   6.6%

C   11. A stock sells for $28; its current dividend is $1.00, and its dividend growth rate is 4.4%. What is the shareholder's required rate of return?

        a.   6.6%
        b.   7.7%
        c.   8.1%
        d.   8.8%

A   12. The dividend growth rate should be calculated via the _____ mean.

        a.   geometric
        b.   arithmetic
        c.   harmonic
        d.   standardized

D   13. To illustrate why dividends do not matter, the text
     used a _____ example.

          a. used car
          b. new car
          c. paint can
          d. shoebox

A   14. Dividend policy is associated with which of the
     following subfields within finance?

          a. signaling
          b. optimum capital structure
          c. market anomalies
          d. technical analysis

D   15. A stock split in which shareholders hold fewer
     shares after the split is a

          a. forward split
          b. direct split
          c. indirect split
          d. reverse split

A   16. The primary motivation for a stock split is usually
     a desire to

          a. reduce the stock price
          b. reduce the dividend requirement
          c. reduce the number of shares outstanding
          d. reduce earnings per share

D   17. A 25% stock dividend is equivalent to a

          a. 2 for 1 stock split
          b. 1 for 2 stock split
          c. 4 for 5 stock split
          d. 5 for 4 stock split

A   18. Blue chip stocks generally

          a. have a long uninterrupted history of dividend
              payments
          b. are not growth stocks
          c. have high dividend payout ratios
          d. have high price-earnings ratios

D   19. A steel company is probably a _____ stock.

      a. blue chip
      b. income
      c. defensive
      d. cyclical

C   20. A retail food company is a good example of a _____ stock.

      a. blue chip
      b. income
      c. defensive
      d. cyclical

D   21. Which of the following pairs of stock categories is mutually exclusive?

      a. income, blue chip
      b. growth, penny
      c. income, defensive
      d. cyclical, defensive

B   22. If a stock symbol contains a period, this means

      a. it trades over the counter
      b. there is more than one class of stock
      c. it is a preferred stock
      d. it trades on the American Stock Exchange

Chapter Eleven

Bond Selection

B   1. Bond price risk is composed of

    a. reinvestment rate risk and market risk
    b. interest rate risk and default risk
    c. interest rate risk and systematic risk
    d. default risk and convexity risk

A   2. Which of the following terms is out of place with bonds?

    a. systematic risk
    b. default risk
    c. reinvestment rate risk
    d. interest rate risk

A   3. All of the following are credit bureaus except

    a. Jones and McLaughlin's
    b. Moody's
    c. Standard and Poor's
    d. Dun and Bradstreet

B   4. If someone seeks to diversify default risk, they need to

    a. buy bonds with differing maturities
    b. buy bonds from different issuers
    c. buy bonds with different coupons
    d. buy bonds with different durations

D   5. In general, the farther out one goes on the yield curve, the

    a. greater the interest rate risk
    b. greater the yield to maturity
    c. greater the duration
    d. all of the above

B   6.   The relation between a bond beta and its duration is

           a.   direct
           b.   inverse
           c.   exponential
           d.   logarithmic

D   7.   A bond which sells at a premium is expected to

           a.   pay interest less than the market averages
           b.   mature sooner than average
           c.   have more default risk than average
           d.   have a higher coupon than average

C   8.   Whether or not a bond sells at a premium is largely
       determined by

           a.   the maturity
           b.   the duration
           c.   the coupon
           d.   the bond rating

C   9.   Which of the following statements is most accurate
       regarding callable bonds?

           a.   Portfolio managers avoid them because of their
                low coupons.
           b.   Portfolio managers seek them because of their
                higher yield.
           c.   Portfolio managers avoid them because of their
                inconvenience risk.
           d.   Portfolio manages seek them because of their
                lower duration.

B   10. The expected return on a bond portfolio can be
       raised by all of the following except

           a.   choosing lower bond ratings
           b.   choosing lower coupons
           c.   choosing longer maturities
           d.   choosing higher betas

A   11. A bond which pays interest on July 15 probably also
        pays interest on

        a.   January 15
        b.   February 15
        c.   March 15
        d.   April 15

D   12. In the Standard and Poor's <u>Bond Guide</u> you see a
        bond identified as the XYZ 11s98. The interest dates
        are listed as Jj. This bond matures on

        a.   June 15, 1998
        b.   July 1, 2011
        c.   June 1, 1998
        d.   January 1, 1998

D   13. A portfolio contains 15 XYZ 11s98 bonds. How much
        will the next interest check you receive from XYZ likely
        be?

        a. $1100
        b. $1500
        c. $1650
        d. $825

B   14. A bond portfolio is constructed so as to pay exact-
        ly $2000 per month in income to the beneficiary. At the
        time this portfolio purchased, the accrued interest
        which must be paid will be about

        a. $2000
        b. $6000
        c. $12000
        d. $24000

C   15. Which of the following was recommended in the text?

        a.   Never buy junk bonds
        b.   Never buy bonds selling at a premium
        c.   Never ask your client for more money
        d.   Never buy callable bonds

Chapter Twelve

Security Screening

B   1. The primary motivation for stock screening is

        a. the efficient market hypothesis
        b. lack of time
        c. lack of research material
        d. the implications of the efficient frontier

C   2. Common screens described in the text include all of the following except

        a. SAT scores
        b. speed in the 40-yard dash
        c. hobbies
        d. bench press ability

D   3. All of the following are characteristics of a good screen except

        a. ease of administration
        b. relevance and appropriateness
        c. acceptance to the user
        d. historical precedent

A   4. An investment service which ranks securities on both timeliness and safety is

        a. Value Line
        b. Moody's
        c. Weissenberger's
        d. Standard and Poor's

A   5. Which of the following timeliness and safety rankings is preferred?

        a. 1,1
        b. 1,5
        c. 3,3
        d. 5,1

A 6. Which of the following publications is published each month with the entire publication conveniently fitting in a briefcase?

    a. S&P <u>Stock</u> <u>Guide</u>
    b. S&P <u>Stock</u> <u>Report</u>
    c. Value Line <u>Investment</u> <u>Survey</u>
    d. Moody's <u>Manual</u> <u>of</u> <u>Investments</u>

D 7. A set of screening criteria dealing with South Africa are the _____ principles.

    a. MacBride
    b. Sutherland
    c. England
    d. Sullivan

A 8. A set of screening criteria dealing with Ireland are the _____ principles.

    a. MacBride
    b. Sutherland
    c. England
    d. Sullivan

A 9. Which of the following is a common screening criterion available from a local newspaper?

    a. the PE ratio
    b. the current ratio
    c. return on assets
    d. times interest earned

A 10. The primary objective of a security screen is to

    a. reduce the security universe in size
    b. find the best potential investment
    c. reduce portfolio risk
    d. increase portfolio dividends

B 11. A quick risk assessment can accomplished by a historical comparison of

    a. current ratio and debt ratio
    b. ROA and ROE
    c. dividend yield and PE
    d. payout ratio and plowback ratio

A   12. Shadow stocks are identified by the

        a. American Association of Individual Investors
        b. Value Line Investment Survey
        c. Standard & Poor's Corporation
        d. Dun and Bradstreet Corporation

C   13. A popular computerized mutual fund screen is pub-
             lished by

        a. Computer Systems, Inc.
        b. American Portfolios Limited
        c. _Business_ _Week_
        d. Dynamic Funds

Chapter Thirteen

The Role of Real Assets

D   1.   Classical characteristics of land include all of the following except

    a.   it is immobile
    b.   it is fungible
    c.   it is indestructible
    d.   it is non-income producing

B   2.   Which of the following is a financial asset?

    a.   gold bar
    b.   stock certificate
    c.   automobile
    d.   office building

D   3.   Which of the following is a real asset?

    a.   corporate bond
    b.   government bond
    c.   twenty dollar bill
    d.   computer

D   4.   _____ property is a legal interest in real estate.

    a.   Personal
    b.   Proprietary
    c.   Financial
    d.   Real

A   5.   Which of the following is a characteristic of a financial asset?

    a.   It has a corresponding liability.
    b.   It produces income.
    c.   It usually shows price appreciation.
    d.   It usually generates no income.

D   6.   The majority of institutional landowners are looking
        for

        a.   annual cash flows
        b.   long-term price appreciation
        c.   short-term price appreciation
        d.   a mix of annual cash flows and long-term price
             appreciation

B   7.   Of their investments in real estate, pension funds
        have about ____ of their money in timberland.

        a.   2%
        b.   4%
        c.   8%
        d.   12%

A   8.   Usual motivations for timberland investment   include
        all of the following except

        a.   regulatory defense
        b.   collateral
        c.   pure investment
        d.   strategic investment

A   9.   State governments with large investments in   timber-
        land are

        a.   California and New Hampshire
        b.   Missouri and Maine
        c.   Alabama and Texas
        d.   Pennsylvania and New Jersey

B   10. Growing trees are called

        a.   land stands
        b.   stumpage
        c.   wood on the hoof
        d.   volume land

C   11. Conditions that make a section of land different
        than the surrounding terrain are called

        a.   biological factors
        b.   fungibility factors
        c.   microsite factors
        d.   acquisition factors

D   12.   A trained forest appraiser knows to look for for
ests undergoing

    a.   a species shift
    b.   a microsite shift
    c.   mutual canopy support
    d.   a product class shift

A   13.   Timberland losses due to fire, insects, and disease
total less than _____ per year.

    a.   0.2%
    b.   2%
    c.   5%
    d.   10%

B   14.   Clear-cutting may be appropriate if a forest de
pends on

    a.   river drainage
    b.   mutual canopy support
    c.   wetland waterfowl
    d.   animal grazing

A   15.   A significant inhibition to timberland investment
is

    a.   the lack of a standard timberland index
    b.   adverse Internal Revenue Service rulings
    c.   high commission costs
    d.   inability to generate income

A   16.   One study indicates that the correlation coefficient between timberland and the S&P500 index is about

    a.   −.50
    b.   0
    c.   .50
    d.   .95

C   17.   A common motivation for the purchase of gold is

    a.   income generation
    b.   tax advantages
    c.   the security it provides
    d.   a substitute for equity securities

D   18.   The price of gold is fixed daily in

           a.   Budapest
           b.   Washington, D. C.
           c.   Amsterdam
           d.   London

A   19.   The largest percentage of privately held gold is in

           a.   France
           b.   the United States
           c.   India
           d.   Saudi Arabia

C   20.   Which of the following is generally not a driving
force behind gold price movements?

           a.   inflation
           b.   the strength of foreign currencies
           c.   supply
           d.   demand

A   21.   The primary advantage of gold certificates is

           a.   convenience
           b.   tax reasons
           c.   added income producing ability
           d.   added security against corporate default

D   22.   For a U. S. coin in circulation, which of the
following is usually highest?

           a.   numismatic value
           b.   intrinsic value
           c.   popular value
           d.   fiat value

Chapter Fourteen

Revision of the Equity Portfolio

B   1. In an active management strategy, the composition of the portfolio is

    a. static
    b. dynamic
    c. determined in advance and not changed
    d. revised very seldom

B   2. A strategy of passive management is one in which, once established, the portfolio is

    a. readjusted on a regular basis
    b. largely left alone
    c. readjusted at the manager's discretion
    d. only readjusted if prices decline

B   3. Naive strategies

    a. should never be used
    b. are not necessarily bad ones
    c. are only appropriate with small portfolios of stock
    d. are seldom in the investor's best interest

D   4. Which of the following is a naive strategy?

    a. constant beta
    b. constant proporation
    c. laddered portfolio
    d. buy and hold

A   5. Common methods of stock portfolio rebalancing include all of the following except

    a. maintaining a constant price earnings ratio
    b. maintaining a constant beta
    c. indexing
    d. maintaining a constant proportion

B   6.   Many investors try to avoid

            a.   blue chip stocks
            b.   odd lots
            c.   no-load mutual funds
            d.   stocks with no beta

B   7.   The purchase of odd lots sometimes involves

            a.   added risk
            b.   a slightly higher commission cost
            c.   a tax disincentive
            d.   slightly lower dividends

C   8.   Round lots are especially important to the

            a.   bond investor
            b.   short-term investor
            c.   option user
            d.   speculator

Chapter Fifteen

Revision of the Fixed Income Portfolio

A   1. Passive bond strategies include

    a. buy & hold, indexing
    b. constant beta, constant proportion
    c. constant duration, constant yield
    d. constant duration, constant convexity

A   2. Which of the following is usually least appropriate for a bond portfolio?

    a. buy and hold
    b. indexing
    c. constant proportion
    d. barbell strategy

D   3. The Handbook of Fixed Income Securities lists _____ different bond indexes.

    a. 9
    b. 29
    c. 129
    d. 229

C   4. A well-known bond index is one published by

    a. Jackson, Brookings
    b. Donaldson, Lufkin, Jenrette
    c. Lehman Kuhn Loeb
    d. Josephthals

D   5. Which of the following is the principal characteristic of a laddered bond portfolio?

    a. constant annual income
    b. constant portfolio value
    c. no interest rate risk
    d. equal proportions across the yield curve

A   6.   Annual revision of a laddered bond portfolio re-
       quires

            a.   buying a long-term bond
            b.   selling a short-term bond
            c.   selling a long-term bond
            d.   buying a short-term bond

B   7.   The principal way in which a barbell portfolio
       differs from a laddered portfolio is the barbell has

            a.   greater investment in the middle maturities
            b.   less investment in the middle maturities
            c.   greater investment in high coupon bonds
            d.   greater investment in low coupon bonds

D   8.   Which of the following is arbitrary in a barbell
       bond portfolio?

            a.   number of weights
            b.   size of the weights
            c.   thickness of the bar
            d.   all of the above

B   9.   If you pay commissions to buy or sell bonds, annual
       revision of a barbell portfolio requires the payment of
       _____ commissions.

            a.   2
            b.   3
            c.   4
            d.   6

B   10. If you hold yield to maturity constant and plot
       bond duration as a function of years until maturity,
       the curve has a _____ first derivative and a _____
       second derivative.

            a.   positive, positive
            b.   positive, negative
            c.   negative, positive
            d.   negative, negative

A   11. Yield curve inversion occurs when

       a.   short-term rates are rising faster than long-term
            rates
       b.   long-term rates are rising faster than short-term
            rates
       c.   short-term rates equal long-term rates
       d.   T-bill rates are less than government bond rates

A   12. Which of the following types of swaps is inconsist-
            ent with the efficient market hypothesis?

       a.   substitution
       b.   intermarket
       c.   bond rating
       d.   rate anticipation

A   13. Convexity is the difference between

       a.   actual price change and duration-predicted price
            change
       b.   actual price change and market average price
            change
       c.   actual price change and government bond price
            change
       d.   actual price change and yield to maturity change

D   14. The importance of convexity increases as

       a.   time passes
       b.   the level of interest rates rises
       c.   the level of interest rates falls
       d.   the magnitude of the rate change increases

B   15. Convexity is related to the ____ derivative of the
            bond pricing relationship.

       a.   first
       b.   second
       c.   third
       d.   fourth

C   16. Modified duration is _____ Macaulay duration.

       a.   equal to
       b.   greater than
       c.   less than
       d.   greater than or equal to

D   17.   Which of the following is false?

        a.   The higher the yield to maturity, the lower the
              convexity, everything else being equal.
        b.   The lower the coupon, the greater the convexity,
              everything else being equal.
        c.   The greater the convexity, the better, everything
              else being equal.
        d.   The higher the duration, the lower the convexity,
              everything else being equal.

A   18.   Everything else being equal, bond investors prefer

        a.   high convexity
        b.   low convexity
        c.   convexity equal to the bond market average
        d.   none of the above

Chapter Sixteen

Principles of Options and Option Pricing

B   1. A famous option pricing model was developed by

    a. Fisher and Lorie
    b. Black and Scholes
    c. Ingersoll and Rand
    d. Sharpe and Lintner

A   2. A primary use of options in portfolio management is

    a. risk management
    b. meeting statutory requirements
    c. satisfying legal lists
    d. estate taxes

B   3. The most common use of options by individuals is

    a. tax avoidance
    b. income generation
    c. arbitrage
    d. diversification

C   4. Which of the following gives its owner the right to buy?

    a. straddle
    b. put option
    c. call option
    d. spread

C   5. The price of an option is called its

    a. time value
    b. intrinsic value
    c. premium
    d. expiration value

D   6. For most options, an individual investor views expiration day as the _____ of the month

    a. first business day
    b. second Tuesday
    c. second Tuesday after the first Monday
    d. third Friday

A   7. Writing an option is

        a. selling an option as an opening transaction
        b. selling an option as a closing transaction
        c. buying an option as an opening transaction
        d. buying an option as a closing transaction

B   8. Who keeps the option premium no matter what?

        a. the Options Clearing Corporation
        b. the option writer
        c. the option buyer
        d. the option writer and the option buyer split it

D   9. A stock priced at $55 per share will most likely
        have option striking prices _____ apart.

        a. $1
        b. $2
        c. $4
        d. $5

B   10. The Options Clearing Corporation is most concerned
        with

        a. market risk
        b. credit risk
        c. interest rate risk
        d. political risk

A   11. On which of the following exchanges are the fewest
        options traded?

        a. New York Stock Exchange
        b. Philadelphia Stock Exchange
        c. Chicago Board Options Exchange
        d. American Stock Exchange

B   12. The book used an example of call options and

        a. libraries
        b. hockey tickets
        c. automobile transmissions
        d. telephones

B   13. Which of the following is correct?

         a. intrinsic value - time value = option premium
         b. intrinsic value + time value = option premium
         c. intrinsic value = time value - option premium
         d. intrinsic value = time value + option premium

D   14. An option which can be exercised anytime is a(n)

         a. European option
         b. wildcard option
         c. Asian option
         d. American option

C   15. An option contract usually covers _____ shares.

         a. 10
         b. 50
         c. 100
         d. 1000

B   16. Option exercise is at the prerogative of the

         a. option writer
         b. option buyer
         c. either the option writer or the option buyer
         d. Options Clearing Corporation

C   17. An increase in which of the following will cause a
      call option to decline in value?

         a. volatility
         b. underlying asset price
         c. striking price
         d. interest rates

B   18. A person holds 2 XYZ APR 60 calls. What is their
      holding after a 2 for 1 stock split?

         a. 2 XYZ APR 60 calls
         b. 4 XYZ APR 30 calls
         c. 2 XYZ APR 30 calls
         d. 4 XYZ APR 60 calls

D   19.   All of the following are assumptions of the Black-
Scholes option pricing model except

    a.   markets are efficient
    b.   no dividends
    c.   interest rates are constant
    d.   investors are generally bullish

B   20.   Delta is

    a.   the theoretical value of an option
    b.   the expected change in the option value as the
       underlying asset price changes
    c.   the intrinsic value of the option
    d.   the influence of dividends on the option value

C   21.   For at-the-money stock options, put/call parity
requires that, for otherwise similar options,

    a.   puts sell for more than calls
    b.   puts sell for the same price as calls
    c.   puts sell for less than calls
    d.   puts sell for at least as much as calls

Chapter Seventeen

Option Overwriting

D 1. The most common motivation for option overwriting is

    a. risk management
    b. tax reduction
    c. leverage
    d. income generation

A 2. If someone writes a call while owning the underling asset, the call is

    a. covered
    b. long
    c. naked
    d. cash-secured

B 3. A long position is a(n)

    a. long-term investment
    b. owned asset
    c. borrowed asset
    d. a position with a paper gain

B 4. If a person writes a covered call with a striking price of $45 and receives $3 in premium, exercise will occur if the stock price is above _____ on expiration day.

    a. $42
    b. $45
    c. $48
    d. $50

C 5. If stock is purchased at $50 and a $55 call is written for a premium of $2, the maximum possible gain per share is

    a. $2
    b. $5
    c. $7
    d. $10

A   6.   If a call option with a striking price of $50 is purchased for $3 1/2, the maximum loss is

       a. $3 1/2
       b. $46 1/2
       c. $50
       d.   unlimited

B   7.   Which of the following strategies has the highest possible loss?

       a.   buying a call
       b.   writing a naked call
       c.   writing a covered call
       d.   buying a put

D   8.   Which of the following terms is least common?

       a.   long call
       b.   short call
       c.   covered call
       d.   covered put

A   9.   Writing a covered call results in a position similar to a

       a.   fiduciary put
       b.   long put
       c.   long call
       d.   long stock position

B   10.   Fiduciary puts are also called

       a.   regulatory puts
       b.   cash-secured puts
       c.   long puts
       d.   uncovered puts

A   11.   If someone writes a put, they usually want the market to

       a.   go up
       b.   go down
       c.   stay unchanged
       d.   fluctuate

B   12. If someone writes a naked call, they usually want
     the market to

         a. go up
         b. go down
         c. stay unchanged
         d. fluctuate

A   13. If someone writes an in-the-money put, they usually
     want the market to

         a. go up
         b. go down
         c. stay unchanged
         d. fluctuate

B   14. If someone writes an in-the-money naked call, they
     usually want the market to

         a. go up
         b. go down
         c. stay unchanged
         d. fluctuate

D   15. Which of the following has the greatest possible
     dollar loss?

         a. writing a covered call
         b. buying a call
         c. writing a fiduciary put
         d. put overwriting

A   16. Index options have little _____ risk.

         a. unsystematic
         b. systematic
         c. market
         d. total

B   17. Which of the following is true for writing index
     calls?

         a. It always increases portfolio market risk.
         b. It need not involve borrowing any money.
         c. It is inappropriate for a tax-exempt investor.
         d. It lowers portfolio income.

A   18.   Which of the following "counts most" in the margin
        equivalents table?

            a.   cash
            b.   US treasury securities
            c.   corporate debt
            d.   stock

D   19.   A person who sought to buy stock at a price below
        the current price might

            a.   buy deep-in-the-money calls
            b.   buy deep-in-the-money puts
            c.   write deep-in-the-money calls
            d.   write deep-in-the-money puts

C   20.   A person who sought to sell stock at a price above
        the current price might

            a.   buy deep-in-the-money calls
            b.   buy deep-in-the-money puts
            c.   write deep-in-the-money calls
            d.   write deep-in-the-money puts

Chapter Eighteen

Performance Evaluation

C   1.   The essence of performance evaluation is

    a. measuring after-tax dollars
    b. associating a measure of risk with expected return
    c. associating a measure of risk with realized return
    d. using the geometric mean whenever possible

B   2.   Expected utility is a _____ function of return and a _____ function of risk.

    a. positive, positive
    b. positive, negative
    c. negative, positive
    d. negative, negative

D   3.   The two mutual funds used in the text example are

    a. Vanguard and Twentieth Century
    b. Fidelity and Strong
    c. Beacon Hill and Pennsylvania Mutual
    d. 44 Wall Street and Mutual Shares

A   4.   _____ are more important than _____.

    a. Dollars, percentages
    b. Paper gains, paper losses
    c. Monthly returns, annual returns
    d. Dividends, capital gains

C   5.   Which measure calculates excess return per unit of total risk?

    a. Jensen
    b. Treynor
    c. Sharpe
    d. geometric mean

B   6.   Which measure calculates excess return per unit of
systematic risk?

        a.   Jensen
        b.   Treynor
        c.   Sharpe
        d.   geometric mean

B   7.   A single security should be evaluated using the
_____ measure.

        a.   Jensen
        b.   Treynor
        c.   Sharpe
        d.   geometric mean

A   8.   The best performance comes from

        a.   highest return per unit of risk
        b.   lowest risk
        c.   lowest long-term volatility
        d.   highest excess return

A   9.   Which of the following performance measures has
statistical problems?

        a.   Jensen
        b.   Treynor
        c.   Sharpe
        d.   geometric mean

A   10. If a portfolio experiences cash withdrawals and
deposits, the best performance measure is

        a.   the internal rate of return
        b.   the payback
        c.   the Treynor measure
        d.   the Sharpe measure

A   11. A common finance assumption which is violated when
options are included in a stock portfolio is

        a.   normality of returns
        b.   constant interest rates
        c.   constant beta
        d.   no taxes

C   12. The incremental risk-adjusted return from options
makes use of the _____ performance measure.

        a.   Jensen
        b.   Treynor
        c.   Sharpe
        d.   geometric mean

D   13. The residual option spread makes use of the _____
performance measure.

        a.   Jensen
        b.   Treynor
        c.   Sharpe
        d.   geometric mean

Chapter Nineteen

Principles of the Futures Market

A   1.   Options are _____; futures are _____.

     a.   rights, promises
     b.   securities, contracts
     c.   paid for, margined
     d.   all of the above

C   2.   The cash price is also called the

     a.   delivery price
     b.   settlement price
     c.   spot price
     d.   bid price

A   3.   The primary economic purpose of the futures market is

     a.   risk transfer
     b.   income generation
     c.   time value of money adjustments
     d.   speculation

A   4.   The clearing corporation helps eliminate

     a.   credit risk
     b.   the risk of crop failure
     c.   the risk of poor crop prices
     d.   liquidity risk

C   5.   Futures trades occur in an area called a(n)

     a.   arena
     b.   ring
     c.   pit
     d.   box

A   6.   The money a futures buyer puts down is called all of the following except

     a.   premium
     b.   good faith deposit
     c.   margin
     d.   performance bond

D   7.   People who seek to reduce risk using futures contracts are

      a.   speculators
      b.   investors
      c.   gamblers
      d.   hedgers

C   8.   In some respects, speculators sell

      a.   time value
      b.   risk
      c.   insurance
      d.   improved credit ratings

A   9.   Someone who routinely maintains a futures position overnight is likely to be any of the following except a

      a.   scalper
      b.   position trader
      c.   speculator
      d.   hedger

B   10.   A major function of the clearing process is

      a.   risk reduction
      b.   matching trades
      c.   finding willing buyers
      d.   finding willing sellers

D   11.   The newspaper price for a particular futures contract is properly called the

      a.   bid price
      b.   ask price
      c.   closing price
      d.   settlement price

C   12.   The prices of some futures contracts are constrained by

      a.   initial margin requirements
      b.   variation margin requirements
      c.   daily price limits
      d.   capital constraints

D   13.   The three main paradigms in futures pricing include
        all of the following except

        a.   the expectations hypothesis
        b.   normal backwardation
        c.   a full carrying charge market
        d.   supply and demand

B   14.   According to John Maynard Keynes, futures prices
        are

        a.   unbiased
        b.   biased downward
        c.   biased upward
        d.   biased either upward or downward

A   15.   The difference between a futures price and the cash
        price is known as the

        a.   basis
        b.   settlement price
        c.   vigorish
        d.   spread

Chapter Twenty

Benching the Equity Players

A   1. Delta enables the portfolio manager to determine

    a. the number of options necessary to mimic the returns of the underlying security
    b. the number of options necessary to reduce the risk of the underlying portfolio by half
    c. the number of options necessary to double the portfolio return per unit of risk
    d. the standard deviation of portfolio returns

B   2. The simultaneous holding of a long stock position and a long put is called a

    a. fiduciary put
    b. protective put
    c. collateralized put
    d. cash-secured put

A   3. For a call option, delta is always

    a. greater than one
    b. less than one
    c. less than one and greater than zero
    d. less than or equal to zero

B   4. For a call option, delta _____ as the striking price _____.

    a. increases, increases
    b. decreases, increases
    c. increases, approaches the stock price
    d. decreases, approaches the stock price

A   5. For at-the-money puts and calls on the same stock,

    a. the put delta is always less than the call delta
    b. the put delta is always equal to the call delta
    c. the put delta is always greater than the call delta
    d. the put delta is always less than or equal to the call delta

6.   When calculating a protective put hedge ratio, all of the following pieces of information are necessary except

    a.   delta
    b.   option striking price
    c.   stock beta
    d.   number of shares of stock held

7.   A characteristic of stock index futures is

    a.   they have limited risk
    b.   they pay dividends monthly
    c.   they are settled in cash
    d.   they have a beta of zero

8.   If the S&P500 index is 400.00, how many S&P500 futures contracts must be sold to hedge a $10 million stock portfolio with a beta of 1.10?

    a.   50
    b.   55
    c.   60
    d.   65

9.   Which of the following statements is true regarding a stock index futures contract?

    a.   the basis is usually negative
    b.   the basis will converge on zero as time passes
    c.   the basis will only decrease; it cannot increase
    d.   the basis will only increase; it cannot decrease

10. Dynamic hedging strategies seek to

    a.   replicate a put option
    b.   replicate a call option
    c.   replicate a covered call option
    d.   replicate a short put

11. A portfolio contains 10,000 shares of XYZ stock; the portfolio manager writes 10 XYZ calls. If the call delta is 0.455, what is the position delta?

    a.   455
    b.   545
    c.   10,455
    d.   cannot be determined

12.   A portfolio contains 10,000 shares of XYZ stock; the portfolio manager buys 10 XYZ puts.   If the put delta is -0.220, what is the position delta?

   a.   220
   b.   780
   c.   10,220
   d.   cannot be determined

13.   An ABC JUN 45 call has a delta of 0.445; what is the delta of an ABC JUN 45 put?

   a.   0.445
   b.   0.555
   c.   -0.555
   d.   -0.445

14.   All of the following will lower position delta except

   a.   buying puts
   b.   buying calls
   c.   writing calls
   d.   selling stock

15.   When futures contracts are used in dynamic hedging, falling security prices will cause the manager to

   a.   buy futures contracts
   b.   buy more stock
   c.   sell futures contracts
   d.   sell stock

Chapter Twenty-One

Removing Interest Rate Risk

C   1. The most important intermediate term interest rate futures contract is on

      a. treasury bills
      b. Eurodollars
      c. treasury notes
      d. treasury bonds

A   2. A Eurodollar is a dollar-denominated deposit

      a. outside the United States
      b. in Europe
      c. in Europe or North America
      d. in Europe, Asia, or the Pacific Basin

B   3. A $10,000 6-month T-bill sells for $9,800. What is its annualized yield to maturity?

      a. 2.04%
      b. 4.08%
      c. 6.12%
      d. 6.66%

D   4. A T-bill futures contract calls for the delivery of

      a. $100,000 of 60 day T-bills
      b. $100,000 of 90 day T-bills
      c. $1 million of 60 day T-bills
      d. $1 million of 90 day T-bills

A   5. If someone had a need to lock in a short-term interest rates, they would be most likely to

      a. buy T-bill futures
      b. sell T-bill futures
      c. buy T-note futures
      d. sell T-note futures

C   6.   Treasury bonds

         a.   are not callable
         b.   may be callable after 10 years
         c.   may be callable after 15 years
         d.   are always callable after 5 years

B   7.   An adjustment factor is used to convert a T-bond to
       a bond yielding

         a.   7%
         b.   8%
         c.   9%
         d.   10%

B   8.   Which is the correct formula for invoice price?

         a.   (settlement price/conversion factor) - accrued
              interest
         b.   (settlement price * conversion factor) + acc.
              interest
         c.   (settlement price/conversion factor) + accrued
              interest
         b.   (settlement price * conversion factor) - acc.
              interest

A   9.   When long-term interest rates are above 8%, the
       cheapest to deliver bond

         a.   has the highest duration
         b.   has the lowest duration
         c.   has duration equal to 15.0
         d.   has the highest yield to maturity

D   10.   Immunization strategies deal mostly with

         a.   credit risk
         b.   market risk
         c.   convenience risk
         d.   interest rate risk

A   11.   In a bullet immunization application, the manager
seeks to get _____ to cancel out.

   a.   interest rate risk and reinvestment rate risk
   b.   interest rate risk and default risk
   c.   convenience risk and price risk
   d.   reinvestment rate risk and default risk

B   12.   If interest rates are expected to rise, the portfolio manager might logically

   a.   raise duration
   b.   lower duration
   c.   lower average yield
   d.   lower average bond rating

D   13.   A bank's funds gap equals

   a.   the extent to which asset duration exceeds li-
        ability duration
   b.   total assets minus total liabilities
   c.   total assets minus current liabilities
   d.   rate sensitive assets minus rate sensitive li-
        abilities

A   14.   Banks usually make duration adjustments by

   a.   altering the left side of the balance sheet
   b.   altering the right side of the balance sheet
   c.   altering both sides of the balance sheet
   d.   altering only the equity account

B   15.   Disadvantages of immunization include all of the
following except

   a.   opportunity cost of being wrong
   b.   it only works for long-term investment horizons
   c.   transactions costs
   d.   it reduces the portfolio yield

Chapter Twenty-Two

Integrating Derivative Assets and Portfolio Management

A 1. Constructing a stock portfolio which meets a set of constraints can be accomplished via

    a. linear programming
    b. calculation of the economic order quantity
    c. finding the net present value
    d. duration matching

C 2. The chapter example generated additional income using

    a. equity calls
    b. equity puts
    c. index calls
    d. index puts

B 3. If index calls are used to generate additional income in a stock portfolio, which of the following statements is true?

    a. Regardless of the portfolio size, the income which can be generated with index calls is fixed and known.
    b. The higher the striking price, the greater the number of options which can be written.
    c. The lower the striking price, the greater the number of options which can be written.
    d. Writing index options eliminates the downside risk of a portfolio.

A 4. Writing calls will always _____ a portfolio's _____.

    a. reduce, beta
    b. increase, beta
    c. reduce, duration
    d. increase, duration

A   5.   A portfolio has a position delta of 1,250 and a beta
     of 1.15.   If calls are written against it such that the
     position delta falls to 500, what is the new portfolio
     beta?

          a.   0.46
          b.   0.55
          c.   1.05
          d.   1.15; beta will not change

B   6.   Implied volatility is a(n)

          a.   estimated statistic
          b.   catchall statistic
          c.   independent variable
          d.   binomial variable

D   7.   Hedging company-specific risk is best done using

          a.   index puts
          b.   index calls
          c.   equity calls
          d.   equity puts

C   8.   The chapter showed an example of using which mathe-
     matical technique in determining the number of puts and
     calls to use in a particular application?

          a.   differential equations
          b.   calculus
          c.   simultaneous equations
          d.   imaginary numbers

A   9.   Which of the following is not necessary in calculat-
     ing a Treasury bond hedge ratio?

          a.   the portfolio yield to maturity
          b.   the portfolio duration
          c.   the duration of the cheapest to deliver bond
          d.   the adjustment factor

D   10. A futures option pricing model is the

          a.   Miller model
          b.   Chance model
          c.   White model
          d.   Black model

Chapter Twenty-Three

Contemporary Issues in Portfolio Management

A 1. Successful implementation of which of the following
is inconsistent with the efficient market hypothesis?

    a. short selling
    b. stock lending
    c. certificateless trading
    d. tactical asset allocation

A 2. The hardest part of a tactical asset allocation
strategy is

    a. asset class appraisal
    b. product class shifting
    c. determining covariances
    d. determining the swing component

D 3. Investment strategies are commonly grouped into all
of the following categories except

    a. anticipatory
    b. reactive
    c. static
    d. variable

A 4. The ideal investment strategy is

    a. anticipatory
    b. reactive
    c. static
    d. variable

B 5. The key element of tactical asset allocation is

    a. duration matching
    b. properly investing the swing component
    c. dollar cost averaging
    d. immunization

B   6.   Short selling involves

          a.   borrowing money
          b.   the sale of borrowed shares
          c.   a bullish outlook on the market
          d.   all of the above

C   7.   Who pays the dividends on borrowed shares that are
          sold short?

          a.   the brokerage firm
          b.   the issuing corporation
          c.   the borrower
          d.   no one

B   8.   Stock lending is facilitated by

          a.   arbitrageurs
          b.   stock loan finders
          c.   investment bankers
          d.   municipal officers

D   9.   An area of abuse in stock lending is

          a.   the loan of shares long-term
          b.   the booking of paper gains
          c.   usurious interest rates
          d.   lending shares held in a cash account

A   10. In a long/short portfolio, the key thing is for the

          a.   long portfolio to outperform the short
          b.   short portfolio to outperform the long
          c.   long portfolio and short portfolio to perform
               equally well
          d.   portfolio to be purchased with cash rather than
               on margin

D   11. A trend in the securities business is toward

          a.   elimination of odd lots
          b.   elimination of stock options
          c.   elimination of futures contracts
          d.   elimination of stock certificates

B   12.   Program trading involves all of the following
      except

            a.   portfolio trading
            b.   dividend capture
            c.   computerized trading
            d.   computer decision making

C   13.   A recent article by Fama and French questions which
      of the following paradigms in finance?

            a.   the efficient market hypothesis
            b.   the time value of money
            c.   beta
            d.   the riskfree rate

NOTES ON PORTMAN AND THE STRONG SOFTWARE

I. GENERAL COMMENTS

A 3 1/2 inch disk is packaged with each textbook sold. If you need a 5 1/4" disk instead, one can be requested through West Publishing by calling (708) 433-2061.

The disk contains two directories: Portman and Strong. To access the Portman program, at the A prompt (A>), type

        cd\portman

 and the computer should respond with

        A>PORTMAN

To look at the Strong Software files, return to the A> and type

        cd\strong

The computer will respond

        A>STRONG

The only reason you would do this is to view the contents of the directory. The Strong Software is Lotus 1-2-3 based, and to access the files you must first load Lotus.

II. PORTMAN

A.   Portman is a stand-alone program; it does not require Lotus or any other software package to run.

        NOTE THAT EXTENSIVE INSTRUCTIONS   ON
        PORTMAN ARE INCLUDED BEGINNING ON PAGE
        544 OF THE TEXTBOOK.

B.   Early model XT's:

If your computer is not equipped with a "true" Hercules compatible graphics card, you may encounter problems booting the software. To solve this, you need a Hercules emulator software program such as HGCIBM. Running HGCIBM will give you the emulation. Most local computer software dealers should sell this or a similar emulator program for less than

$5.00, and will sometimes provide one free.

At the A> prompt, load this emulator software before running Portman.

C.   If you have trouble loading Portman:

You may want to check the "color" file by typing:

TYPE COLOR <ENTER>

It should read:

      8
      20 _____ for VGA Color

OR

      2
      20 _____ for CGA Color

To change the color file, type:

COPY CON: COLOR <ENTER>

      (For color monitor)

      8 <ENTER>
      20 <ENTER>
      CNTRL-Z <ENTER>
OR

      (For CGA non-color)

      2 <ENTER>
      20 <ENTER>
      CNTRL-Z <ENTER>

D.   Running Portman

In constructing portfolios, Portman is sensitive to miss-ing information. If, for instance, you prepare a portfolio but omit dividend or beta information, the program may solve the problem on the computer screen but not allow you to save the portfolio.

If you want to ignore dividends and want to save your work, it is necessary to actually select the DIVIDENDS PER SHARE option and accept the default value of 0. Similarly, if you want to ignore beta, you may find it best to enter 0 for each security's beta.

In order to save portfolios to disk, the disk cannot be write-protected. Ensure that the write protect tab is in the correct position.

III. STRONG SOFTWARE

The Strong Software is Lotus 1-2-3 based. You must first access Lotus and change the Lotus file directory to the drive where the Strong Software disk is located. For instance, if you have Lotus loaded on a hard disk (a C: drive) and put the software disk in the A drive, after calling Lotus up, use the sequence of Lotus commands

        /file directory a:

Lotus will then check the disk in the A: drive and list the files on the Strong Software disk. To use one of the files, use the Lotus command sequence

        /file retrieve

followed by the name of the file you want, or you can high-light the file name with the cursor and ENTER.

Many of the Strong Software files contain a Lotus macro; these are all involved by simultaneously depressing the ALT key and S. Macros will not run if you have menu items at the top of the page; hit the ESC key until the Lotus menu clears.

Some files have their own menus, which I programmed. These can be used anytime. Macros also run while these are displayed.

The COV file, which calculates covariance and correlation matrices as well as individual security statistics, is large. If you have attached a Lotus add-in such as WYSIWYG, some computers will run out of memory while using the COV file. To get around this, simply select the "add-in" option from the Lotus menu and DETACH WYSIWYG. This frees memory and the COV file will run.

The Duration file uses a convergence macro to find duration and yield to maturity. At the bottom of the screen is a "seed number" which should be copied into the hidden cell as indicated in the on-screen instructions. Doing so increases the speed of solution dramatically. On a slow computer, failure to do this can cause the computer to spend up to five minutes searching for a solution. (On a 386 or 486 computer ignoring the seed is not much of a problem.)

The BONDPORT file provides for the input of the months in which bonds pay interest. This information is entered with the letters of the months. A bond which pays interest in February and August, for instance, would be entered as fa or FA (lower case or upper case). You must, however, enter the months chronologically. February comes before August, so the "f" comes first. Entering AF will not produce an error message, but interest in those months will be omitted.